COLOMBE PRINS
ANTHONY ZAMECZKOWSKI

#FANS

UNDERSTANDING THE NEW HYPER-CONNECTED GENERATION ON SOCIAL MEDIA, INCLUDING YOUTUBE, TWITTER, INSTAGRAM AND VINE

TRANSLATED BY MARTIN HOFFMAN

To our dear ones,
To all Millennials,
To the fans.

Preface by editorial director

Since time immemorial, artists have had supporters who have followed them from exhibit to exhibit, from concert to concert and from show to show. The exponential growth of the internet has vastly expanded the expressive realm of fans, who can now give free reign to their enthusiasms on the various social networks. Fans were quick to realize the multimedia power of the web and soon began to use it not only to express what they thought about their favorite stars but also to showcase themselves on easy-to-launch blogs, on video hosting sites (YouTube in particular) and then on Facebook, Twitter, Pinterest, Instagram, Snapchat, Tumblr, Periscope and other platforms. They learned to take selfies and send snaps (via Snapchat) and progressively became reporters, photographers, comics and teachers.

Suddenly something quite surprising occurred : from among their own ranks, web users discovered genuine stars who had something to say, and who moreover were saying it in a way that truly spoke to their target audience. Beginning with tentative forays into self-expression, these up-and-coming web personalities quickly developed a considerable audience who then developed into a community of fans, who in turn converted their friends... The multiplier effect of networks functioned so marvelously well that in the blink of an eye this new medium gave birth to genuine stars. Suddenly television—the king of all media—and its stable of stars started to appear old hat, as did print media and even e-mail.

The owners of the new internet media companies were quick to analyze how they could leverage the relationship between artists and their fans by putting in place systems to monetize their audience, in the form of advertising.

Anthony Zameczkowski and Colombe Prins are well placed to chronicle the rise of internet-driven fan culture. Anthony was a member of YouTube's initial team during the launch of the video sharing platform in France in June of 2007, only three years after the company was founded in the US. According to Le Journal du Net, a possible reason why YouTube chose France as the first country outside of the US to expand its operations is that YouTube recognized the growing clout of its French competitor, Dailymotion. In fact, at that time the two video sharing platforms were neck and neck in the French market, each with nearly 5 million unique visitors per month. Google—YouTube's parent company—therefore gambled on launching a localized French-language version of the platform in the hope of gaining the upper hand over its French competitor... a gamble that paid off!

These days on YouTube some 400 hours of video are uploaded every minute, nearly 6 billion hours of video are viewed every month, and the most watched video of all—with more than 2.3 billion views—is « *Gangnam Style* » by South Korean singer Psy.

Throughout this book, we discover the names and websites of online personalities who, thanks to the astounding amount of web traffic they generate, have become world famous stars in fields as varied as fashion and make-up, the movie industry, cooking, comedy, music, video games, etc.

I myself have experienced the giddiness that the immediacy of the internet can inspire when, through pure serendipity, my friend PPC and I launched « *Les Vidéos du Succès* » [1] (« *The Videos of Success* »). Our first video, on how to become a good photographer, was shot more than eight years ago when I was on a flight with a group of seven other French geeks, on our way to visit Silicon Valley. [2] Our second video, on the topic of « *winning résumés* », was shot at a gas station in San Francisco and the third, which deals with managing e-mail when you're traveling, was shot on a cable car in the same city. The fourth, on the topic of « *losing weight without dieting* », was shot in a McDonald's in Paris. Many more were to follow. Indeed, over the past eight-plus years, PPC and I have shot more than 400 videos which together have been viewed 13,200,000 times! The internet is akin to the Wild West: he who plants his flag first gets the land.

This book, which reads like a novel, is being published on the occasion of the 10th anniversary of the founding of YouTube.

Happy Birthday, YouTube!

Henri Kaufman
@henrikaufman

1 https://www.youtube.com/user/VideoPeps/videos
2 This video, which has been viewed more than 100,000 times, was uploaded at San Francisco International Airport because there happened to be Wi-Fi where we were waiting to pick up our rental cars.

Foreword by Jean-Marc Tassetto

A former Managing Director of Google France and SFR, Jean-Marc Tassetto is one of the co-founders of Coorpacademy, a start-up specializing in on-line training for companies.

The Third Industrial Revolution is digital. Just as the first two revolutions, beginning at the end of the 18th century, contributed their share of inventions such as the steam engine and electric power, the recent digital wave is transforming 21st century society and individual behavior, even going so far as to meet a fundamental need that had been as-yet unfulfilled. Thanks to the internet and social networks, people can satisfy their need to socialize and be connected to others. It is easier than ever for them to have discussions and exchanges with like-minded individuals whom they trust. Now more than ever, people are inclined to believe less in institutions or elites and to believe more in those with whom they are close and who share their interests.

These are exciting times we live in: vertical structures are transitioning to horizontal ones. Communication, which until recently was based on a hierarchical, quasi-military model, is evolving towards exchanges among equals. This need for horizontality also finds expression in «*low-profile*» architecture. Our modern-day Empire State Buildings no longer scrape the sky; the headquarters of Google and Facebook are constructions on a human scale.

This Third Industrial Revolution, which could be summed up by the catchphrase «*power to the people*», is restoring autonomy and a sense of community to the individual. The direction of history at the beginning of this century has been marked by a trend towards freedom in which each individual seeks fulfillment. Internet users surf the web in search of topics that interest them and inspire their involvement.

In 10 years, YouTube has become a veritable search engine, thereby bringing video into the culture of the new connected generations. This titan of online video has contributed in a major way to the transformation of behaviors by creating, through its many channels, a genuine phenomenon of community and collaboration.

By inventing the short video format, YouTube enabled new content creators to express themselves and gave power to the new fans of the 21st century. What we are witnessing is a momentous revolution.

In a connected world, social networks, which allow free access to speech, information, knowledge, intercommunication and skills, channel the hopes and dreams of the Millennials—the generation born with the new technologies of connectivity. The internet opens the frontier of possibilities and offers opportunities to all in a multitude of sectors.

Education and teaching—two areas that are particularly close to my heart—are now accessible in the four corners of the world thanks to the web. We call these online classes « *MOOCs* » : massive online open courses that are open to all. These new online educational platforms stoke students' curiosity through a pedagogical approach that is more interactive and personalized. Students choose the subjects that interest them and progress at their own pace, as their abilities and availability allow. They are free to browse, to dabble here and there and to delve deeper into certain topics. In addition, the content of e-courses is bolstered by attractive media such as video and social networks.

Traditional teaching methods stifled students' strong appetite for knowledge by forcing them to listen passively to teachers dictating their lessons. Lecture halls were empty because professors were reading out research articles that their students had already read at the library. Now classrooms are surprisingly full thanks to online learning. In fact, students familiarize themselves with a subject by studying it first on a screen before posing questions directly to instructors, who are rediscovering their true role. Students want teachers who impart their knowledge, who inspire, who delve deeper and who make them feel like learning.

The École Polytechnique Fédérale (Federal Polytechnic School) of Lausanne is an example of a university that has more than 50,000 students taking the same class together. No more classrooms: students are now meeting in stadiums. Just as fans flock to the concert of a singer they idolize, e-students attend the classes of their favorite teachers.

Online courses also stimulate students' appetite for courses taught by teachers in person. The digital realm and physical reality are therefore not so disconnected from each other. On the contrary, the former stimulates demand for the latter.

The digital realm inspires emotion, and every generation is touched by it. Naturally, for Millennials, who have grown up with these technologies, the internet is something they take for granted. But it is also a new playground and source of information for older generations. The internet neither siloes nor segments; the web is universal.

Did you know that...?

- On any given day, there are 1.13 million daily active users on Facebook.[1].
- Each month, nearly 6 billion hours of video are viewed on YouTube.[2]
- Every minute, 400 hours of video are uploaded to YouTube.[3]
- Every day, 500 million tweets are sent.[4]
- The most watched video on YouTube, with more than 2.3 billion views, is the official video for "Gangnam Style" by South Korean singer Psy.[5]
- Katy Perry is the most followed person on Twitter, with more than 93 million subscribers.[6]
- There are more than 1 million content creators who earn money from their YouTube videos.[7]
- More than 95 million photos and videos are shared every day on Instagram.[8]
- Netflix represents 35% of internet bandwidth usage in North America. [9]
- The valuation of Snapchat, which was founded in 2011, was estimated at around 20 billion dollars in 2016.[10]

1 Facebook, June 2016.
2 DMR, April 2014.
3 Tubefilter.com, July 2015.
4 Twitter, March 2015.
5 YouTube, August 2015.
6 Twitter Counter, October 2016.
7 YouTube, 2015.
8 Instagram, 2016.
9 Variety, November 2014.
10 Bloomberg, May 2016.

Introduction

All of us either are or have been the fan of a celebrity.

What is a fan, or "otaku" as the Japanese call them? Fans are admirers. They feel a fervent passion for a movie star, a singer, a band or an athlete, and know more about the object of their devotion than just about anyone else.

They go to the concerts of their favorite musical stars and to the games or matches of their favorite sports stars, and they buy all sort of products emblazoned with their likeness. In the past, they belonged to fan clubs that communicated through the mail and they subscribed to printed fanzines. Nowadays they stay abreast of news about their favorite stars on social networks, subscribe to their YouTube channels and follow them on Instagram and Twitter. Fans have a direct, personal and authentic relationship with these celebrities.

Fans have been around for a long time. The word "fan", which is actually an abbreviation of the word "fanatic", entered the lexicon towards the end of the 19th century. So why write a book about fans now, given that they are hardly a recent phenomenon?

The reason is that the nature of fandom has considerably evolved in recent years thanks to new technologies and online platforms that have given them much more power and influence than they once had. These days, fans "like", tweet about, share, comment on, subscribe to and follow what interests them, and some of them even fund the creators of this content.

A major evolution that one might even call a revolution is underway. How have these new technologies empowered fans? How have the latter revolutionized the media landscape and so much more? And what lessons can we draw from this ongoing revolution so that we can better understand and communicate with the fans of the Millennial generation?

My name is Anthony Zameczkowski and I was born in Paris in 1978. My parents both worked in the media industry. They initially ran their own record label, as well a specialized music industry magazine, and later on they moved in to the television industry. My grandfather also worked in media. He established the first megastore in France, called Nuggets. He also founded the Jazz à Juan jazz festival in Juan-les-Pins and Jazz Magazine, both of which are still going strong. I have always been one of his greatest admirers.

As a child, I met more than a few celebrities and fans. I was myself a huge fan of Michael Jackson, Genesis and Stevie Wonder.

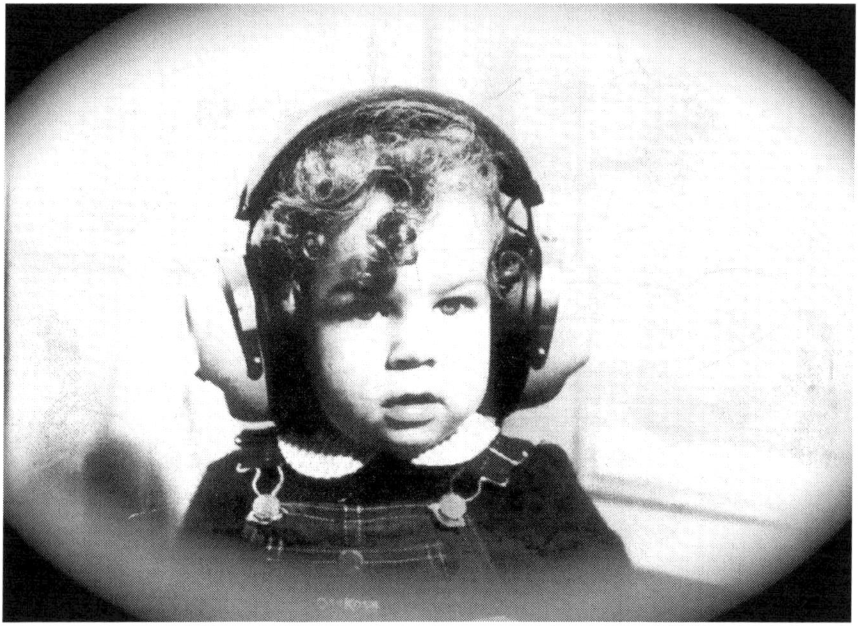

Anthony Zameczkowski at the age of 3

After graduating from business school in France, it was natural for me to maintain the family tradition of working in media. In 1999, I was hired by the Lagardère group in France to sell television programs to markets outside of France.

At the time, the internet was not well developed in France and we still communicated with clients by fax. The company had a single e-mail address which was shared by all the employees, using a dedicated computer. Google was still an unknown startup, and watching a video on the web was a real feat.

1999 and 2000—before the dot-com bubble burst—were crazy years when many entrepreneurs were seeking investments to launch a new technology startup. Anybody with a half-baked business plan could raise significant sums. These new companies were so overvalued that America Online (AOL), an internet services company, managed to buy out the media giant Time Warner.

It was in October 2000, the month of the merger, that I joined this major new corporation, AOL Time Warner. It was deemed to be the biggest merger in the history of the world. A few years later, it was also deemed to be the most disastrous. AOL Time Warner mistakenly thought it would be able to reinvent the media universe. Ultimately, the revolution that did happen some 10 years later was not the doing of the traditional media groups but rather the achievement of a mobilized, active and connected audience, i.e.: FANS!

After six years at Time Warner as head of program sales to European television networks, I had the good fortune in 2006 to be hired by Google to handle the development of Google Video in a number of European countries. Unfortunately, this on-demand video site was not as successful as had been hoped. Google therefore decided to buy the market leader, YouTube, for $1.65 billion—one of the biggest acquisitions the search engine company had ever made.

At the time, this seemed like an insane gamble. YouTube was a young California startup that had only been in existence for 19 months, but its success had already been quick and phenomenal. The site allowed anybody to view videos very quickly and share their own clips with the whole world. I was one of the first YouTube employees to work outside of the United States. I still remember the first time I visited YouTube's offices in San Bruno. At the time, the startup had only 75 employees. They had yet to realize the extent to which YouTube was going to change the world in just a few years.

The company did not have a real business model and its reputation had been sullied by a number of lawsuits alleging copyright and piracy violations. For the media industry, YouTube was seen as public enemy number one. I had the difficult task of convincing media groups and professional sports organizations to work with us to distribute their content. Our meetings were sometimes quite tense. Often, rather than meeting with the people in charge of digital content, I found myself face to face with lawyers who wanted to sue us for copyright infringement. Moreover, my peers in the profession as well as my own family couldn't understand how I could «betray the business" by working for "pirates".

Those in the traditional media who had a short-term vision of YouTube failed to imagine the potential of the world's leading online video-sharing platform. Most of them sued YouTube or, at best, ignored it. In 2007, I was put in charge of negotiating an agreement with the English Premier League, which is the largest soccer league in the United Kingdom. Following the failure of these negotiations, the league, together with the Viacom media group, decided to file a class-action lawsuit against YouTube. This resulted in my being interrogated in New York for more than 10 hours by attorneys representing both Viacom and the English Premier League as part of this lawsuit, in which the two complainants were claiming $1 billion in damages. The English Premier League and Viacom were convinced that YouTube was inciting users to put pirated content online and was profiting from it. Of course that was not the case at all: most users were only using the site to share their own amateur videos, such as the now famous one of a dog riding a skateboard.

YouTube has now become a global video-sharing platform that is recognized the world over. In January 2013, I was the director of YouTube Music for the Asia-Pacific region, and in that capacity I received on behalf of YouTube a prize awarded by the Corea Image Communication Institute, thanking us for having played a role in the success and international popularity of South Korean singer Psy, famous for his song "Gangnam Style".

YouTube now has real influence and can generate considerable income both for individual content creators and industry professionals. The video-sharing platform, as well as social networks like Facebook, Instagram and Vine, have allowed new stars to emerge and sometimes have even sparked revolutions, such as during the Arab Spring.

There is no doubt that an economic and social upheaval is underway in the media industry and beyond. The question is: Where does it currently stand?

Chapter 1 – Technologies: a new tool for fans

«In recent years, the acquisition [of YouTube by Google] has looked like a steal as more YouTube stars have reached mainstream popularity and more advertisers flock to the platform.»

Garett Sloane, journalist, writing for Adweek[1] magazine.

1 Article published in September 2014.

In the world of traditional media as it has existed for decades, solely broadcasters and production companies have been able to produce content, to broadcast it and to manufacture celebrities. In this industry, the barriers to entry are numerous and the amount of investment required is apt to discourage new players in the market. For example, a television network must hold an official license to be allowed to broadcast its programs. The audiovisual industry is heavily regulated and these regulations are a guarantee for the television networks to earn profits by limiting competition.

In the traditional system, viewers are passive. Even if they have the impression that they are choosing what to watch, surfing from channel to channel with the remote in hand, the choice of content is imposed on them.

However, the development of new technologies is changing these habits. Viewers are no longer just spectators: they interact, they like, they share and they comment. They choose what to consume and produce what they want to share. Henceforth, there are no more economic or technical barriers to sharing content on the internet. Producing a video using a computer, a mobile phone or a camera has become widely accessible. For example, more than 10 years ago, a video camera might cost around $5,000, whereas today a $200 smartphone is enough to produce a video of the same quality.

Now broadcasting is within everyone's reach. Using video platforms such as YouTube, Vimeo, Dailymotion, Youku[1], Niconico[2] and Vine, it is possible to share content free of charge with the entire world. In 2015, approximately 400 hours of video[3] were uploaded every minute to YouTube. From parodies to cooking demos to the latest trendy music video—not to mention the high-jinks of cats and dogs—everything can be found on the web.

1 Youku is the Chinese equivalent of YouTube.
2 Niconico is the Japanese equivalent of YouTube.
3 Tubefilter.com, July 2015.

YouTube: the origin of the «fan system»

YouTube was launched in 2005 by Steve Chen, Chad Hurley and Jawed Karim, three former employees of PayPal, the online payment site. What is now the world's largest video-hosting platform was originally supposed to be a dating site, according to Mashable, a website specializing in news about the web and social networks. Ultimately, however, the trio did not follow that path. The first video posted to the site was produced by Jawed Karim, one of the platform's three founders, and features his comments during a visit to the San Diego Zoo. His video, "Me at the zoo", is still online and as of October 2016 it had been viewed more than 34 million times.

Link to the video «*Me at the zoo*»:
https://www.youtube.com/watch? v=jNQXAC9IVRw&list=PL0Om7-9U86ZWi2jldSAVyAf8GIUtYRmzz

In 2006, the California start-up was bought by web giant Google for $1.65 billion. At the time, YouTube suffered from a poor reputation, having been accused of piracy and copyright infringement—problems that industry analysts said would mean the demise of the young company. The memory of the forced shutdown in 2001 of Napster, a site specialized in the illegal downloading of music, remained fresh in people's minds.

But the company that was said to be doomed nearly 10 years ago has now become a colossus of online video and much more. YouTube has undoubtedly made history by revolutionizing the media industry as well as the day-to-day lives of hyper-connected young people.

YouTube now has more than 1 billion unique visitors every month. In the beginning, the company had fewer than 100 hundred employees. Ten years later, the video-sharing platform is localized in more than 88 countries and has more than 1,500 employees worldwide.

Much of YouTube's success has also been tied to major technical innovations that have allowed users to load videos faster, and with better image quality, with each passing year.

From the advent of the mobile era...

Until the new millenium, most internet users only got online via a stationary computer using a wired connection. Surfing the web was a static activity and for many the connection was billed by the minute. Remember the sound of a dial-up modem connecting to the internet?

These days, our mobile devices are the primary screen through which we surf the web. « *Smartphones allowed more than 3 billion people to access content* », explains William Bao Bean[1], a venture capitalist who invests in new technologies. « *Phones really opened up the world.* »

Their smartphone is their best friend.

Approximately 50 % of the views on YouTube are via a mobile phone[2]. Going on the internet has become an ordinary thing that people do while they're out and about. During every waking hour, users constantly visit websites and check their messages and various social media accounts. In 2007, with the invention of the touch screen and its iOS technology, Apple revolutionized people's internet habits. Since then, Android, a rival operating system developed by Google, has also become dominant on the market. With their little icons,

1 Interviewed by the authors in January 2015.
2 Think with Google, The YouTube Insight team, April 2015.

cell phones have become a smart tool—hence the «*smartphone*» moniker—and just as powerful as a computer. In 2014, 4G enabled high bandwidth connections for mobile phones, which facilitates web surfing in general and the viewing of YouTube videos in particular.

... to the disappearance of the television set

In a world in which telephone screens are growing in size, television sets are becoming less indispensable. Some even say the «*small screen*» of the TV, with the features it has today, is destined to disappear. Reed Hastings, the CEO and co-founder of Netflix, which streams movies and TV series over the internet, made the following announcement in a manifesto published in 2013: «*Over the coming decades and across the world, internet TV will replace linear TV. Apps will replace channels, remote controls will disappear, and screens will proliferate.*»

Pay TV is already the first to undergo this evolution which is only accelerating, and which is causing it to lose some of its prestige. By way of example, according to a study carried out in the United States between March and May of 2014 by Nielsen Video Census and Nielsen People Meter, YouTube already reaches 18- to 34-year-olds more than any cable TV network. An article published in the Wall Street Journal in November 2014 revealed that the pay TV industry had lost 222,000 subscribers that year in the United States.

Cable television companies, which sell their customers bundles of channels, are being bypassed by viewers' desire to only watch the programs they choose, at the times that suit them. Why should they subscribe to a bundle with a multitude of channels when they will only end up watching a few of them?

More and more, viewers want to «*cut the cord*» to the television set so that they can discover new worlds and new ways of consuming images, which is now possible via the internet. We speak of OTT (over-the-top) content, i.e., content that is not sent through a cable TV network but rather via an internet connection, phone, tablet, smart TV, computer or even a video console (such as the PlayStation 4, Xbox One or Wii U), as well as via other connected «*boxes*» such as the Apple TV.

The on-demand video services offered by Netflix and its competitor Hulu have been hugely successful. For less than $10 a month, Netflix subscribers in the United States have access to a catalog of more than 100,000 titles online. Given the success of on-demand video, some traditional TV networks announced their ambition to also make their content available to stream starting in 2015. In October 2014, Richard Plepler, the Chairman and CEO of HBO, explained that « *It is time to remove all barriers to those who want HBO.* » [1] At the same time, CBS announced its intention to move forward with the same strategic choice.[2] Are we now at a turning point in the broadcasting of TV programs?

Netflix: out to conquer the world

Created in 1997 by Reed Hastings and Marc Randolph, Netflix originally offered a system for renting DVDs that allowed members to choose discs online, receive them by mail and watch them without a time limit. The only limitation was the number of DVDs that subscribers could have in their possession at the same time. In 2002, Netflix, which had 600,000 members, launched an IPO in the United States. In 2007, it introduced streaming via its website. Within the space of only a few years it became a global juggernaut of the subscription-based on-demand video industry. Following the launch of this new business model, Netflix's share price took off and the company's market capitalization, currently estimated at $26 billion, increased ten-fold in eight years.

Bolstered by its success in the United States, Netflix set out to conquer Canada, Latin America, the Caribbean and Europe. In 2016, Netflix had more than 86 million subscribers in 190 countries who every day watched more than 125 million hours of TV programs and movies. [3]. The California-based company has also ventured into the financing and production of original content such as movies, series and documentaries, thereby seriously disrupting the audiovisual industry worldwide. Netflix productions include the renowned American series House of Cards and Orange Is the New Black. In 2016, Netflix invested $5 billion to produce its original programs.

1 Time Warner press release, October 15, 2014.
2 The Guardian, October 16, 2014.
3 Netflix, October 2016.

The predominance of social networks

Consumers no longer consider television to be the only source of screen-based content, knowledge and information. They now surf, search and browse on the 'net. The media environment has been disrupted and that of social networks is fragmented between Facebook, Google+, Twitter, Instagram, Snapchat, Pinterest, Tumblr, YouTube, Vine, Dailymotion, Vimeo, Spotify, Youku, Niconico, VKontakte (the « *Russian Facebook* »), etc. Each of these applications offers a wealth of possibilities.

« *When we are thinking about technology and platforms and how they are empowering fans, they are really doing three things* », explains Ted Wright[1], the CEO of Fizz, a marketing agency specializing in word-of-mouth marketing. « *They are allowing exploration, which can be good or bad depending on what it is that you are exploring, they allow for a less expensive sharing and they allow for a much faster transmission of information to a broad number of people.* »

Fans are those who go looking for what interests them on the web and who forward it to their friends. Web surfers control the way in which they share information. And they do so free of charge, quickly and easily! For William Bao Bean[2], « *Traditional content companies are in the business of creating wonderful content but the distribution of their content is done by somebody else. What happened with the internet is that creators were empowered to not only create the content but then also to drive the distribution themselves. Creators connect directly with fans and the fans can engage directly over social media.* » It is these celebrated social networks that are now the primary information distribution channels for the planet.

Facebook no longer needs introducing. Ten years after the social network founded by Mark Zuckerberg went online, it was estimated to have more than 1.47 billion active users connecting to it every month. Notwithstanding, more than a decade into its hegemony on the web, the California-based social network has begun to fall out of favor with the younger generations, who consider it to be unfashionable. Connected teens now prefer other platforms such as Twitter, Instagram and Snapchat, which are less frequented by their parents and grandparents. Indeed, that is why Facebook bought Instagram

1 Interviewed by the authors in January 2015.
2 Interviewed by the authors in January 2015.

in 2012 for a billion dollars. Instagram is a photo-sharing application with approximately 500 million users[1], i.e., more than Twitter, which has 313 million. The other preferred platform of those under the age of 25 is Snapchat, which was launched in 2011 and already has 150 million users.[2]

Among the various social networks there are local and regional differences. Weibo, for example, is considered to be the «*Chinese Twitter*». This micro-blogging site, which was created in 2009, was reported to have approximately 261 million monthly active users as of 2016. In Russia, a different social network predominates. Created in 2006, VKontakte reportedly has more than 100 million users located throughout the countries of the former USSR. Originally, the site was directed primarily towards students. Later, following in the footsteps of its American counterpart, Facebook (which also sports a blue and white color scheme), it widened its target audience. Line is a Japanese social network that combines the best features of a number of other platforms. Three years after it was launched in 2011, Line was reported to have more than 218 million monthly active users who, in addition to sharing content via the platform, can simultaneously use it to make free phone calls and send messages. It is the most popular social network in Japan and has even set out to conquer new markets in Asia, Latin America and Europe.

In the words of a teenager from South Africa who was interviewed by the authors: «*I think we have all the social networks we need and I believe we should stop inventing them because we're probably going to blow up the internet.*»

1 Statista, June 2016.
2 We should mention in the legend that Ted Wright and William Bao Bean have Interviewed by the authors in January 2015.

Pinterest, the creative app

Millennials know that, just as Twitter users «*tweet*», Pinterest users «*pin*». It means to pin a photo on one's «*wall*», i.e., on one's personal Pinterest profile. This new photo app had 150 million monthly active users in 2016 according to Forbes.. Launched in 2010 by Ben Silberman (a former Google employee), Evan Sharp and Paul Sciarra, Pinterst currently has more than 30 billion «*pins*».

Pinterest is not a social platform in the strict sense of the term because its users do not highlight themselves but rather browse among photos searching for all variety of novelties, new interests, inspiration and surprises. Currently valued at more than 11 billion dollars, Pinterest is a prime example of a sharing or «*curation*» application through which fans of handicrafts, decoration, fashion and cuisine can share their good ideas in the form of images.

Snapchat, the giant of ephemeral content

Launched in 2011, the Snapchat application allows users to send photos or videos that vanish after a few seconds. Users themselves determine the length of time that their friends can view the images they send them.

Evan Spiegel and Bobby Murphy originated this concept when they were students at Stanford University in California. They are now billionaires and quite confident about their invention. In 2013, they rejected Facebook's $3 billion purchase offer. Snapchat, which was valued at $10 billion in 2014 and $20 billion in 2016, has also been courted by Google and by Tencent Holdings, a Chinese fund.

Snapchat is the preferred social tool of those under the age of 25, who are always keen to protect their e-reputation. Using Snapchat, they leave no trace behind on the web. Or at least that's what they think: screenshots are still possible, even in under 10 seconds.

The company knows how to evolve by adding features, and that is undoubtedly what pleases its users. It is now possible to tell short stories using images, and to create one's own ultra-short films. A new feature called «*Discover*» gives users access to a new kind of information portal. It features media content in the app's ephemeral format, provided by various news organizations such as CNN, Vice, MTV, National Geographic, Yahoo News and others.

SnapChat has been hit by hackers a number of times. In January 2014, the data of 4.6 million Snapchat users was disclosed, and in the fall of the same year thousands of photos were made public.

KEY TAKEAWAYS:

Through new technologies, Millennials are connected, or even ultra-connected, every hour of the day. Always on the go, they connect to the internet and social platforms when and where they please.

They also play an active role in choosing the content they wish to view, to such an extent that they are even becoming creators and broadcasters themselves.

Chapter 2 – Who are the new fans?

«I would encourage you not to worry so much about how many people watch what you make. Worry about how many people love what you make.»

John Green, author of *The Fault in Our Stars*, @Vidcon 2014.

They call them the Millennials or «*digital natives*». But some prefer to speak of the «*Net Generation*», and still others suggest the terms «*Generation Y*» or «*Generation C*» for the «*connected generation*».

There is no shortage of catchphrases to define this demographic group born at the beginning of the 1980s—the first to have lived their entire lives during the successive introduction of video games, personal computers, mobile phones, the internet and other spin-offs of those technologies, which are completely integrated into their lifestyle. Indeed, when a group of teenagers with multiple social network accounts were asked the question «*What would a world without the internet be like?*», one 13-year-old German girl[1] replied «*I don't know, but I don't want to live in that world!*»

As early as 2001, the American sociologist Marc Prensky coined the expression «*digital natives*», whom he contrasted with «*digital immigrants*», i.e., those who were not born during the digital era and have had to learn how to use computers at a later age.

A study carried out by the U.S. Census Bureau and published in April 2016 by the Pew Research Center reveals that this year the Millennials overtook the Baby Boomers as the largest demographic group in the United States. Those born between 1981 and 1997 numbered about 75.4 million in 2015, while those aged between 51 and 69 numbered about 74.9 million.

What is the typical profile of this generation?

Generation C is defined more by an attitude, a state of mind or a mentality than by a date of birth. For more than half of Generation C, the internet is their primary source of entertainment. According to information provided by Google, 66 % of them spend at least as much time watching videos online as they do watching television[2]. They›re online, most often via their mobile phone, and they are also multitaskers. Even while watching the TV set they check Facebook or other social networks on their smartphones. According to an IPSOS study carried out for Google during the fourth quarter of 2014, 75 % of 18- to 34-year-olds are doing other things while in front of the TV. In contrast, only 50 % of them are distracted while watching YouTube.

1 Interviewed by the authors in March 2015.
2 Gen C YouTube Audience Study, March 2013, Google/IPSOS/Nowwhat.

You could almost say Millennials are impatient: they jump from one video to the next and prefer ones that are short or even very short. Immediacy has become the norm. They want to be able to connect whenever they want, wherever they want, using any computerized device. They absorb information quickly. They read, they watch, they share, like and comment, they tweet and retweet—all in order to create connections and relationships with others, with a community.

Generation C is defined by four C's: connection, creation, community and curation. YouTube has put together a profile of a typical member of Generation C, based on data gathered via its online platform.

1. **Connection:** From morning to evening, and even in the late hours of the night, the youth of Gen C are always connected. Approximately 91% of them sleep with their phone on or next to them.[1] They watch what they want, when they want. Millennials use multiple screens and switch from one device to another many times during the day.

2. **Creation:** They are creative and inventive. Approximately 65% of them have already uploaded a video they've recorded themselves, and 25% of them post a video every week.[2] The content they put online is either original or a remake or reimagining of an existing video. One example is the song «Happy» by Pharrell Williams, countless parodies of which have been produced throughout the world for various occasions.

3. **Community:** They feel the need to belong to a virtual community. Most of them are signed up with multiple social networks. Approximately 55% of them are «friends» with at least 100 people through their accounts[3].

4. **Curation:** Naturally, they share what they like. 90% of them say they can't keep content they like to themselves. 70% say that the content they find online provides them and their friends with subjects of conversation.[4] Each person tries to be the first to inform his or her friends in order to be seen as an opinion leader. Online sharing is a positive attitude and is part of the engaged

1 Google, 2012.
2 Gen C YouTube Audience Study, March 2013, Google/IPSOS/Nowwhat
3 Ibid..
4 Ibid

mindset of Generation C. In the words of Kiera, age 14: «If I like it, I share it. If I don't like it, I don't write any comments.»

Fans during a concert... Smartphones replaced lighters.

Audience vs. Fanbase

As the internet and social networks have developed, the definition of media success has evolved. Although audience figures are still scrutinized, analyzed and dissected minute by minute, they are no longer the only indisputable proof of a program's success; now the number of likes, comments, shares, views and tweets must also be taken into consideration.

More than an audience to be reached, there is now a «*fanbase*» to be won over, i.e., a group or a community of fans. What is the difference between an audience and a fanbase? An audience turns on the television, sits down and consumes. A fanbase chooses the content it wants to watch and when to watch it, and it also interacts. An audience changes the channel when the program is over. A fanbase keeps the show going by sharing and commenting. An audience is national whereas a fanbase is global.

What is a fan?

A fan is a person who feels strong admiration for a movie star, a famous singer, a band or a top athlete. «*Being a fan means already identifying as one*», explains French sociologist Gabriel Segré, author of the book Fans de... Sociologie des nouveaux cultes contemporains.[1] The behavior of Elvis Presley fans is one of the areas of expertise of this research professor. He explains classic fan behavior as follows: «*In many cases, being a fan means knowing everything about a star's life as well as their work. It also entails traveling to see the star in concert, attending fan meetings or gatherings, sharing one's passion with other fans, converting others to one's passion, showing one's emotions with great fervor, [and] talking about the star as if they were a loved one*».

There are countless fans of Michael Jackson, Madonna and The Rolling Stones who belong to fan clubs and who sport t-shirts with the effigy of their icon. But these stars are undoubtedly the idols of a generation of people over the age of 40. Young Generation C has its own stars, its own fans and its own ways of doing things

From offline fans to online fans

«*With new technologies, there have been certain changes in fans' attitudes or an intensification of existing ones*», explains Gabriel Segré. Nowadays, using social networks, stars send messages to their fans and keep them more informed about their private lives than ever.» The close relationship between the fan and the star has thereby been strengthened.

Before fans became connected via today's technologies, meeting up, sharing their passion and gaining awareness of their strength required a good deal of effort and often entailed some travel. «*Nowadays, meeting up, becoming a force and developing a sense of belonging to a group has become far easier due to communication via social networks. In a few clicks, fans can decide on an action or a meetup... Real-time information is expanding considerably*», explains Mr. Segré.

1 Gabriel Segré, Fans de... sociologie des nouveaux cultes contemporains (Paris: Armand Colin, 2014).

Just as the fans of Hollywood stars join fan clubs, in the digital age, groupies also develop a sense of belonging to a group. They even give themselves nicknames. The fans of Bethany Mota—a 20-year-old American Youtuber[1] who gives fashion and makeup advice on YouTube—call themselves «*Motavators*»; those of Jérôme Jarre—a Frenchman who posts comedic sketches on Vine—are «*Jerhomies*»; and fans of the band One Direction are «*Directioners*».

Thanks to social networks, web fans have strengthened their power and influence to such an extent that, in the words of Patrick Walker, Former CEO of Rightster and current Director of Media Partnerships, Europe, Middle East and Africa at Facebook, they are more than fans, «*they are participants*». Rightster is a multi-channel network (MCN) that optimizes and monetizes video content posted on platforms such as YouTube. According to this specialist, who was responsible for YouTube's European partnerships until 2013 and who helped launch the platform in Europe, «*[Web fans] are more engaged than [regular] fans. [...] In a digital environment, your reaction, your like, your thumb up, your forward, your share [...] is a participation in the storytelling process [...] because the reaction is immediate. It helps direct where the story goes.*» He adds that «*people feel a real powerful sense of intimacy [...] like they're friends. [...] Which is why the brands see them as being so important, and why you have a different level of connectivity between these stars and the stars of old who are on the silver screen or on the big screen, because people saw them as being a thought leader or an iconic fashion leader, but they didn't see them as their friend.*» For Patrick Walker, «*It's the combination of that power of the connectivity between the creatives and the participants, the fans, that makes them such a transformational phenomenon that we've never seen before.*»

In that spirit, YouTube—an online video platform created by and for fans—has decided to make video recording studios available to fans who are also content creators. These studios, called YouTube Spaces, will be in a number of major world cities and are already operating in Los Angeles, New York, São Paulo, London, Paris, Tokyo, Berlin, Mumbai and Toronto. The tagline of YouTube Space is «*Bringing together the most creative people in the world to learn, connect and create*». The idea is to allow the owners of YouTube channels that already have a following to improve the content and quality of their videos by providing them free access to production

1 Youtubers are content creators on YouTube.

stages, professional image advisors, lighting specialists, sound engineers and experienced makeup artists, as well as access to post-production facilities. In this way, YouTubers can collaborate and share information with the community of online creators.

Younger and younger fans

The children of fans are in turn becoming fans of online content. Phones and tablets now the favorite objects of young children who, through mimicry, start touching screens with the tips of their little fingers, sometimes even before they learn how to walk.

At the beginning of 2015, Vine, a mobile video platform owned by Twitter that allows users to share looping six-second video clips, launched a new concept dedicated to children. The Vine Kids application, with simplified features, aims to provide fully-secure video content for young children. Close on their heels, Google responded by launching a new children-only application in the United States, YouTube Kids.

Children and even babies are becoming a target audience that is already online. In France, a publisher of children's magazines, Bayard Presse, launched a YouTube channel in March 2014 named after one of its little characters, « *Petit Ours Brun* » (« *Little Brown Bear* »). In over two years, its videos generated more than 245 million views. One of the Petit Ours Brun compilations even became YouTube's third most-viewed video in France in 2014, with more than 16 million views, a number surpassed only by Norman and Cyprien, two French YouTube stars.

Usually at the behest of their parents, have become YouTube stars. At the age of 10, Evan is undoubtedly one of the platform's youngest celebrities. His channel, EvanTubeHD, created in 2011, has more than three million subscribers. Evan's specialty is toys and video games. He likes to comment on, unwrap, try out and build all kinds of toys. three years ago he videoed himself opening and trying out a toy used to make clay models of the Angry Birds. The video has been viewed more than 73 million times. Encouraged by his success, Evan has launched two other YouTube channels: EvanTubeRAW, which features little scenes with him and his family, and EvanTubeGaming on which he has video game matches with his father.

Toy makers are quite taken with Evan and send him free toys in the hope that he'll talk about them in his videos. Spin Master, a Canadian company, even hired Evan to appear in an ad promoting a line of spy-themed toys called Spy Gear. According to Spin Master, Evan's reviews increased the sales of their toys by 65% in 2014. In September 2014, Business Insider, an online magazine, reported that Evan earns approximately $1.3 million per year from his videos posted on YouTube.

Link to Evan's YouTube channel:
https://www.youtube.com/user/EvanTubeHD

Fans and video trends

On YouTube, «*unboxing*» or unwrapping a product has become a trend. These videos feature people commenting as they open presents or packages. This may sound uninteresting, but what has become the art of unboxing delights millions of fans. According to Google, videos featuring unboxing were viewed more than 1 billion times in 2014, and the number of views increased by 57% between 2013 and 2014. In fact, it would take more than seven years to watch all the YouTube videos with the word «*unboxing*» in their title. Fans are especially fond of videos featuring the unboxing of toys, electronic equipment and new technologies like smartphones and tablets. These objects are «*undressed*», as it were, in front of the camera. What's behind the infatuation with these types of videos? Viewers are mainly interested in getting a closer look at the product in its original packaging, without any advertising hype. But beyond that, they feel as though they too are getting to open the product. In addition to unboxing, «*haul*» videos are all the rage online. These generally feature young women showing off the clothes they just bought themselves on an afternoon shopping spree.

KEY TAKEAWAYS:

For Millennial fans, living their lives online is more than a necessity: they simply take it for granted. They are inventive, they create their own content and share it online, and they build a digital community with whom they share what they see, hear and read on the web. Four words sum up this generation of fans: connection, creation, community and curation.

#FANQUOTES

Below is a sampling of comments posted by fans on their Twitter accounts, addressed to their favorite stars:

@BethanyMota
« CANT WAIT TO MEET YOU & TALK TO YOU IN PERSON »

@BethanyMota
« I MET MY INTERNET BESTFRIEND »

@pewdiepie
« It would be awesome if you tell me what you think about my fanart ❤ LOTS OF LOVE FROM BRAZIL »

@MichellePhan
« We found your book Mish !! 😍 all the love from the Philippines ✨ »

« Enjoying @MichellePhan's book at the airport while waiting to board !!! Such a valuable guide !! I really recommend it ! »

@LindseyStirling
« I'm glad you feel better now !;) i hope you like this pic :) greetings from México !!! »

@RosannaPansino
« I tried to make the Lego cake.It was a fail because my cake kept crumbling.I love your videos tho »

These messages written by fans to celebrities are friendly and even loving. The words posted are simple and spontaneous. They prove that a true interaction exists between fans and stars.

#STARQUOTES

And here are a few tweets written by web stars on their Twitter accounts:

Felix Kjellberg @pewdiepie

http://tinyurl.com/hmxoe7h

« Sorry no video yesterday. Car broke down and a bunch of other bs I had to deal with. Back today ! »

Lindsey Stirling @LindseyStirling

http://tinyurl.com/oyxx444

« Sorry, I didn't mean to scare everyone with my snapchat. My body had other plans. Still in the hospital but no worries, I will be home soon. »

 Lilly Singh @IISuperwomanII

http://tinyurl.com/nwj4mgh

« Sometimes I feel like you're the only thing keeping me sane. »

Rosanna Pansino @RosannaPansino

http://tinyurl.com/o46xy2w

« Happy Friday Everyone ! I just finished my last book and am looking for a new series to read. Any suggestions ? »

Ryan Higa @TheRealRyanHiga

http://tinyurl.com/prma6vc

« Need your help for a vid ! Who are some of your favorite mainstream actors these days ? »

YouTube stars express themselves with the same kind of spontaneity and simplicity as their fans. They all speak the same language. There's no fakery or tricks. Their relationship, being based on authenticity, is a relationship of trust. Stars speak to a community that they've built around themselves: a group of friends, a circle of fans.

Chapter 3 – How do fans in turn become stars?

« We [YouTube stars] have this intense emotional connection with our fans. In Singapore they waited outside my hotel and cried when they saw me. »

Lilly Singh, a Canadian YouTube star also known as Superwoman, quoted in *Newsweek*[1]

1 Article published in October 2014.

PewDiePie, Bethany Mota, Nash Grier, Smosh, Lilly Singh... these names barely register with people over the age of 30 (unless they are parents of a teenaged fan) but for Millennials they are a big deal and have become genuine role models.

According to an article published in the Daily Mail in October 2014, nearly 40 % of 16- to 25-year-olds say they want to become a YouTube star, whereas only 6 % of the same age group wish to become a reality TV star.

Famous ...

The stars of YouTube, Vine and Instagram are true celebrities in the hyper-connected world of the under-30 set. They attract millions of people—i.e., subscribers—who follow not just their work but also every single bit of information about them that is posted on online networks.

Their fame is such that it is even spreading beyond the web platforms that gave rise to their stardom. These stars have nurtured close relationships with their fans and feel very close to them.

According to Jasper Donat[1], the organizer and president of YouTube FanFest[2], «*Authenticity and accessibility are the two keywords in the relationship between creators and their fans. Their message is so authentic. These stars don't lie and their fans would do anything they say. Influencers like Bethany Mota [who has more than 10 million followers] are making a good living from product recommendations, but they would never recommend a product they don't like.*»

When Jasper Donat organized the first YouTube FanFest in Singapore in 2013, he was surprised to see «*how creators have built their relationship with their fans*», adding that «*A fan is the most important thing on the planet and almost more important than creators themselves. The creators would do nothing to upset their fans and the creators will go out of the way to meet as many fans as they can.*»

A study carried out and published by Variety magazine in July 2015 revealed that the favorite stars among 13- to 17-year-olds are

1 Interviewed by the authors in December 2014

2 YouTube FanFest is an event gathering the most popular YouTube stars for a few days. Since 2013, the event happened in Singapore, India, Australia, South Korea and Japan.

Youtubers, who have effectively dethroned Hollywood stars such as Will Smith and Johnny Depp. For some celebrities, YouTube is an end unto itself, granting access to unimaginable fame, and for others it is a springboard to new horizons, a way of pursuing their dreams in a different way.

... and rich, thanks to YouTube

Stars who have found their fame on YouTube have also made a fortune thanks to the online video platform. In 2007, YouTube established a partnership program with content creators. The Partner Program, which is now active in more than 90 countries, allows content creators to monetize their online videos by way of ads or subscriptions. Specifically, YouTube automatically places video ads or banner ads before, or even during videos. Viewers can then choose to watch them or ignore them, but only after a minimum of five seconds of viewing. YouTube pays more than half of ad sales revenue to content creators, who own the rights to their own videos.

There are now more than 1 million content creators who earn money from their YouTube videos. According to the company, which is an affiliate of Google, thousands of channels individually generate more than $100,000 in revenue every year.

The VidCon Revolution

Created in 2010 by two brothers, Hank and John Green, who are both vloggers (video bloggers), VidCon is a gathering that brings together YouTube stars and their fans for several days of concerts, shows and discussions in Anaheim, California. The event aims to be at the center of the ongoing web revolution.

As stated by the VidCon website: "We believe deeply that we are in the very early, defining moments of an extremely powerful global force. VidCon strives to be the physical center of that revolution."

In 2010, VidCon attracted 1,400 participants. The 2016 conference welcomed nearly 25,000 attendees and more than 300 YouTube stars.

The event has given rise to a number of offshoots in various countries, including the YouTube FanFest in Asia, Summer in the City in England, VideoDays in Germany and Video City in France.

Who are these web stars?

Michelle Phan

Michelle Phan taking a selfie with her fans in April 2014 in New York.

At the age of 30, Michelle Phan achieved worldwide fame on the web for her makeup tips. She currently has nearly 9 million subscribers to her YouTube channel. Since 2007, this young Vietnamese American vlogger has been sharing her passion for makeup by posting online tutorials featuring beauty tips. She is also known for making herself up as a skeleton, as Daenerys Targaryen—heroine of the TV series Game of Thrones, as the humanoid persona «*Hatsune Miku*» of Japan, and even as Lady Gaga. In fact, her video entitled «*Lady Gaga Bad Romance Look*» has been viewed more than 54 million times. Beyond her success with her admirers, Michelle Phan is also sought after by major cosmetics brands. In 2010, she became a video makeup artist for Lancôme and in 2013, with the support of L'Oréal, she launched her own line of cosmetics, called em, with more than 250 items. Last year she published her first book, Make Up. And in 2012 she founded ipsy, a service that mails subscribers a bag of 10 beauty and makeup products every month for $10 per month. A veritable queen of the beauty scene, Michelle Phan has built a multi-million dollar empire.

Link to Michelle Phan›s video introduction:
https://www.youtube.com/watch? v=bHVOxhEpjp0

Hikakin Kaihatsu

Hikaru Kaihatsu, better known by the name Hikakin, is a 27-year-old Japanese beatboxer. Using nothing but his own voice, he reproduces the sounds of various musical instruments. Four years ago he became famous for his interpretation of the music to a Super Mario video game. The video has scored more than 36 million views on his YouTube channel, which has more than 1.8 million subscribers. Hikakin has beatboxed with major international stars such as Aerosmith and Ariana Grande, and covered famous songs like «*Let It Go*» from the film Frozen, Daft Punk's «*Harder, Better, Faster, Stronger*» and Eminem's «*Not Afraid*». In 2013, he decided to diversify by creating a new channel focusing on video games, called «*HikakinGames*», which currently has more than 2.3 million subscribers.

Link to the «*Super Mario Beatbox*» video:
https://www.youtube.com/watch? v=LE-JN7_rxtE

Lindsey Stirling

Lindsey Stirling, who has a following of more than 8 million people on YouTube, plays hip hop on the violin. In 2010, she was a contestant on America's Got Talent, which she left following her performance in the quarterfinals. Piers Morgan, one of the three judges, told her: «*You're not untalented, but you're not good enough to get away with flying through the air and trying to play the violin at the same time.*» To this, Sharon Osbourne, one of the other judges, added: «*You need to be in a group. [...] What you're doing is not enough to fill a theater in Vegas.*» The young violinist, who was 23 at the time, decided to post her videos on the internet. They were a big hit. Fans adore her style and she cultivates the art of using novel settings. Her videos are shot in wide-open spaces, often out in nature, including forests, the countryside, the beach or the African savannah. She is unstoppable, and her ever-growing audience love her originality and authenticity.

Her video « *Crystallize* », which was posted in 2012, has been viewed by 158 million people, making her a genuine online phenomenon. Her self-titled album has sold more than 350,000 copies in the United States without even being backed by a major label, and has become a platinum record in Germany and a gold record in Poland and Switzerland. In another video, set in a forest, she dresses up as Link, the main character of the video game series The Legend of Zelda. It has been viewed more than 30 million times. And her cover of the Japanese song « *Senbonzakura* », originally recorded under the moniker of virtual singer « *Hatsune Miku* », reached 1 million views within its first week on YouTube.

For the past two years, Lindsey Stirling has been performing at sold-out concerts around the world and Forbes magazine listed her as one of the « *30 Under 30 in Music* » for the year 2015. Revenge has been sweet for this one-time quarterfinalist of *America's Got Talent*.

Link to the « *Lindsey Stirling America's Got Talent* » video:
https://www.youtube.com/watch? v=M2xL7D5IPAk

Jérôme Jarre

This 25-year-old Frenchman has been living in the United States for nearly three years and has become a social network star, especially on Vine, a mobile application that allows users to post looping six-second videos. He is best known for his short sketches featuring passers-by on the street. What started as a lark for his own amusement has made him a star in America and beyond, with more than 8.5 million followers. Many of his fans, nicknamed « *Jerhomies* », even travel to meet him in person. Flashing his perfect grin, he has also made videos with celebrities such as Robert De Niro and Pharrell Williams. According to an article published in AdWeek magazine, which featured him on its cover in September 2014, some Jérôme Jarre videos are sponsored by large corporations. The magazine reports that the going rate for one of his Vine videos is $25,000 and for a Snapchat message it's $35,000.

Link to the video::
https://www.youtube.com/watch? v=GB3pUV0fJuo

Rosanna Pansino

Rosanna Pansino is a 31-year-old American who has been passionate about pastry and cooking ever since she was a little girl. In 2010, she began uploading videos every Tuesday of her cooking show, Nerdy Nummies, to her YouTube channel, which has 7 million subscribers. On her show she cooks and decorates all variety of cakes. It has become one of the most popular cooking shows online. Her trademark is her penchant for cakes shaped like her favorite animated characters, including Hello Kitty, the Angry Birds, Spider-Man, Super Mario and SpongeBob.

Her reason for creating a YouTube channel was to train herself to speak more comfortably in front of the camera, because initially she was working as an extra in commercials and movies. Very quickly she received positive feedback and her subscribers began clamoring for new content. Since then she has equipped herself with a full complement of kitchen and video equipment, and now devotes several days to the shooting and post-production of each of her videos, which she enjoys working on with her family members, especially her sister.

Link to the video:
https://www.youtube.com/watch?v=q53HUAKB9oU

Zach King

Zach King, nicknamed «*Vine King*», has truly become the king of special effects on the micro-video platform Vine. This 26-year-old American is followed by nearly 4 million people. In 2008, he began using his website, www.finalcutking.com, to share video editing tips. And on YouTube he began posting his videos, presented as a form of digital wizardry. Five years later, his magic tricks made him a celebrity when he began posting his videos on Vine. Among other high jinks, he takes viewers by surprise by jumping into his car without even opening the door (or window), by pulling an actual cat out of a picture of one on his computer, and by turning his goldfish green. Zach King also gets a sizeable number of laughs from the more than 16 million fans who watch his videos on Instagram. «*Actually I don't really call them fans, I call them friends*», explains the young comedian. «*When they are watching you on their screen, or they are inviting you into their house and into wherever they are, in their car, their school, they are very close to you, so they feel like your friends. And you realize that they want a hug, a handshake, they want a personal touch.*» To go where his fans are, he has toured the United States and even Kuwait. « *I think our success really grows quicker on Vine* », he says, « *because of the style and a lot of short stories I wanted to tell, and I think Vine is a perfect platform for that. The looping feature is also a cool aspect because people can watch the videos three or four times.* »

Link to a montage of Zach King sketches:
https://www.youtube.com/watch? v=cii2JFHGpEk

YouTube stars also like to collaborate with each other and produce new content together. It's just one more way for them to attract new fans while having fun. For example, when 21-year-old style maven Bethany Mota is on the road, she is always eager to meet up with accomplices and make funny videos with them. She has shot a video in Australia with Troye Sivan, whose channel has more than 4 million subscribers, as well as in India with Scherezade Shroff, a local celebrity with whom she has danced to Bollywood beats.

When YouTube artists appear together in a video, it's also a way for them to do cross promotion. That's what Lindsey Stirling did when she appeared in the video for the song « *Come With Us* » featuring the singer Can't Stop Won't Stop and a whole panoply of other YouTube celebrities, including MysteryGuitarMan, EppicTV, Tiffany Alvord, Freddiew, WhatsUpElle, Black Nerd Comedy, Kaleb Nation and Shay Carl.

Link to the video « *Come With Us - Lindsey Stirling & Can't Stop Won't Stop* »:
https://www.youtube.com/watch? v=0HJoNXWWMuA

Interview with Henri Kaufman[1]

Henri Kaufman is the editorial director of the publishing house Éditions Kawa. Since 2007, he and his associate Pierre-Philippe Cormeraie, aka PPC, have been running the YouTube channel « Les Vidéos du Succès » (« The Videos of Success ») which has more than 23,000 subscribers. Their slogan is « 7 good tips in under 7 minutes to succeed in your professional AND personal life ».

How did you decide to do videos on YouTube?

I was on a flight with a group of eight French geeks. We were on our way to visit Silicon Valley. When my friend PPC saw my camera, he asked me for some advice on how to take good pictures and then he said: « *Hey! I'm going to film you!* » So then right away I imagined seven tips in seven minutes on « *how to become a good photographer* ». We shot this on the plane, then PPC edited the video with credits and a soundtrack. As soon as we arrived at the airport in San Francisco and were able to connect to the internet, PPC uploaded it to YouTube. By the next day we already had some views. The day after that, PPC asked me: « *What if we did another video?* » So when we were in front of a gas station we did one on « *winning résumés* ». It was really windy, so I put on an orange baseball cap I'd bought the day before. It ended up becoming this iconic thing in our videos. We shot our third video on a cable car in San Francisco. The theme was « *managing your e-mails efficiently* ». Once we were back in Paris we wondered whether we should keep making more videos, and since people were watching them we decided to keep making them. Over the past eight years we've produced more than 400 videos and they've been viewed by more than 12 million people. What interests me is sharing my advice with people rather than keeping it to myself.

What's behind the success of your YouTube channel?

The first thing is that we benefited from a good network of friends who shared our videos from the get-go. But then what helped us was our steadfastness and our tone. For the last eight years we've come out with a video every week, always with a new subject that will interest somebody. We're known for our good attitude and even our crazy laughter. Even though our subjects are always serious and have to do with issues people ask questions about, we keep it light. We have a

1 Interviewed by the authors in October 2015.

script but there's a good deal of improvisation. We do the shoots in public places. PPC gives as good as he gets. It's lively! These aren't instructional videos filmed from behind a desk. It's just the two of us having a good time. Our fans are treated to a show but also get answers to the questions they've been wondering about. In order to set a good pace, we decided to structure each video with seven topics in seven minutes, because any longer than that took much too long to load—back then, anyway—and was way too tiring for viewers.

What's your view of YouTube stars?

By making videos, YouTube stars invented not just a new style of entertainment but also gave entertainers a whole new outlook. Now everyone can become a star overnight as long as they have an interesting topic and know how to carry themselves in front of a camera. Audiences can be much larger on the internet than elsewhere, so that opens more possibilities to artists than the prospect of selling out a venue.

Link to the video:
https://www.youtube.com/user/VideoPeps?spfreload=1

KEY TAKEAWAYS:

Fans want to develop an authentic, trust-based, intermediary-free relationship with the celebrities they worship. They hope to be able to get in touch with them directly and interact with them. In this way, fans and stars communicate sincerely and even become friends.

The keyword is authenticity. These stars have a close relationship with their audience and are not placed on a pedestal. Communication with Millennials is expected to be authentic.

Chapter 4 – Fans: overcoming the barriers of time and space

« Clearly, the success of the Netflix model—releasing the entire season of House of Cards at once—has proved one thing: the audience wants the control. They want freedom. If they want to binge—as they've been doing on House of Cards—then we should let them binge »

Actor Kevin Spacey, in a lecture given at the Edinburgh Television Festival in 2013.

Until recently, a typical TV viewer's evening was organized as follows: the news at 8: 00 and a movie at 9: 00, followed by a police drama series or a late-night talk show. However, with the boom in video sharing sites such as YouTube and subscription video-on-demand sites such as Netflix, time constraints have been done away with, and immediacy has become the rule. Why wait a week to watch the next episode of your favorite series when you can watch entire seasons of it on the internet without even downloading them, at whatever time you please?

Jimmy Kimmel, who hosts Jimmy Kimmel Live! nightly on ABC, decided to create a self-titled YouTube channel in order to broadcast his show on the internet, thereby reaching a wider audience. His bet has paid off. His channel now has more than 8 million subscribers and his famous video, posted in 2011, in which he asked parents to film their kids' reaction when they told them they had eaten all their Halloween candy, has racked up more than 57 million views. Many others have chosen to share content from their programs online in order to increase their audience and fame. TV programs now have a life beyond their broadcasting timeslot. Thanks to the internet, all content is available all the time, everywhere. In a connected world, geographic barriers have become meaningless.

Link to the video «*I told my kids I ate all their Halloween candy*»: https://www.youtube.com/watch? v=_YQpbzQ6gzs

Borders have vanished

Audiences are no longer limited to the borders of a country, they are global. The success of the video for «*Gangnam Style*», posted on YouTube in 2012 by South Korean singer Psy, is the most significant example of an audience that has now become completely global. Over the course of four years, more than 2.6 billion people watched the singer's video on YouTube's video-exchange platform. The «*horse dance*» craze swept the planet in just a few months, and the video inspired countless parodies. «*Psy's 'Gangnam Style' video became viral to the point of insanity*», explains Bernie Cho[1], the President of DFSB Kollective, a South Korean agency specialized in distributing Korean music around the world. «*Psy flipped the script by proving skeptics wrong on what 'works' overseas. First, Psy was able to show that a Korean act, an Asian act, for that matter, any international act can have a worldwide hit that isn't 100 % in English... but in all fairness, hooking listeners with the 'Hey sexy lady' line probably didn't hurt in the least bit. Second, he galloped along with other trending K-pop [Korean pop] stars who were hopping, skipping and jumping into new overseas markets by deftly using global social media platforms to promote his music—and his videos—worldwide. And third, he was an older, cheeky, very 'well-rounded' artist whose over-the-top worldwide hit not only took him to the top of the charts worldwide but also shattered the stereotype that a global K-pop star [...] should be young, cute, and thin.*» For Bernie Cho, the reasons for the success of Psy are that, «*Despite his age and appearance and in spite of some letdowns and setbacks, Psy's imperfections may have been the perfect reason why he became so endearing to curious fans around the globe. Whether he was sauntering on red carpets or shimmying on talk shows, he was spontaneous, smart, and witty—he came across as someone 'real', not as something 'rehearsed'. Part of Psy's appeal worldwide may be due to his aura of authenticity. Definitely not a one-trick pony, he is actually a triple-crown artist who writes his own music, produces his own music and performs his own music.*»

1 « Interviewed by the authors in January 2015.»

Psy's official YouTube channel when its music video "Gangnam Style" crossed 1 billion views.

Link to the « *Gangnam Style* » video:
https://www.youtube.com/watch? v=9bZkp7q19f0

A mere five years ago, Korean pop music was still little known internationally. Most K-pop videos were viewed within Asia. But since the success of « *Gangnam Style* », more than 90 % of K-pop videos are watched outside of South Korea.[1] « *In the history of K-pop, there is now a before Psy and an after Psy* », notes Mr. Cho. « *Hallyu* », which means « *Korean wave* », is a new term used to describe the exportation of Korean culture. Even though there are only about 80 million people who speak Korean, the entire planet has been won over by K-pop. Currently, the biggest fan club in the world is that of a Korean pop group, TVXQ, who even made it into the Guinness Book of World Records in 2008. In this connected world, language is no longer important and no longer impedes intercultural exchange: videos are watched and listened to the same way the world over.

The number one export market for K-pop is North America, followed by Japan, Southeast Asia and China. According to Bernie Cho, « *What's fascinating about the K-pop music industry is its evolution*

1 BBC: online article dated June 2, 2015.

from 'made for Korea' to 'made in Korea' to 'made by Korea'. Rewind to the 1990s: K-pop was 'made for Korea', available only to Koreans in Korea. Hit pause in the early 2000s: K-pop was 'made in Korea' as big K-pop hits and big K-pop stars started to become big among Asians all across Asia. Now push fast forward and press play in the 2010s: K-pop is more and more 'made by Korea' because, although K-pop artists may be based in Korea, many K-pop albums are composed with international producers, written with multilingual lyrics, sung by multinational members, recorded in overseas studios, and debut on worldwide music charts.» This explains why, on average, 60% of YouTube channel views don't originate from the country in which each channel is based.[1]

KEY TAKEAWAYS:

In a connected, globalized world, time and space have ceased to be the impediments they once were. New creations jump borders to rendezvous with the rest of the world, and circumnavigate the planet in a matter of hours. Visually striking content easily lends itself to exportation, which probably explains the success of the «Gangnam Style» video. Content freed of cultural or linguistic barriers is more easily shared by the fan community, which itself is no longer confined by national borders.

1 The Guardian: online article dated April 8, 2014.

Chapter 5 – Fans: redefining the music industry

« The future of the music industry is a two-way interaction. »

Alexander Ljung, co-founder and CEO of SoundCloud, an online audio platform, in March 2014.

A new way of listening to music

According to a study published by Nielsen in July 2014, around 79 % of the population of the US listens to music online. The CD has become retro. YouTube videos have replaced TV videos and streaming sites have dethroned radio. Music is discovered on the web, which is also where people listen to it, watch the videos for it and share it. Fans have revolutionized the music industry. Increasingly, music is being rented rather than purchased. There is no shortage of music platforms, including Spotify, Deezer, SoundCloud, Rhapsody and others. These applications offer expansive catalogues of songs under license by record companies. They have free versions with advertising and also paid versions for those who wish to avoid ads.

Launched in 2008, Spotify currently dominates the music streaming industry. It has more than 100 million active users, including 40 million subscribers to its "Premium" formula. This Swedish company provides a gateway to more than 30 million songs, and its services have been localized in 60 countries.

Unsurprisingly, many musical artists take issue with these music platforms, which they criticize for shortchanging their work and talent by making their music freely available. Artists such as Taylor Swift and Björk have even decided to withdraw a number of their songs from the Spotify catalog, at the risk of disappointing their fans who have become used to free access. In November 2014, in reaction to the departure of Taylor Swift from Spotify, Daniel Elk, the company's CEO, made the following statement on his blog : « *Taylor Swift is absolutely right : music is art, art has real value, and artists deserve to be paid for it. We started Spotify because we love music and piracy was killing it. So all the talk swirling around lately about how Spotify is making money on the backs of artists upsets me big time. Our whole reason for existence is to help fans find music and help artists connect with fans through a platform that protects them from piracy and pays them for their amazing work. Quincy Jones posted on Facebook that 'Spotify is not the enemy ; piracy is the enemy'. You know why ? Two numbers : zero and two billion. Piracy doesn't pay artists a penny – nothing, zilch, zero. Spotify has paid more than two billion dollars to labels, publishers and collecting societies for distribution to songwriters and recording artists. [...] We're trying to build a new music economy that works for artists in a way the music industry never has before. And it is working – Spotify is the single biggest driver of growth in the music industry, the number one source of increasing revenue, and the first or second biggest source of overall music revenue in many places. Those are facts.»*

Deezer and the «French touch»

Deezer, a site that legally offers free, unlimited music streaming, was launched in 2007 by two Frenchmen: Daniel Marhely and Jonathan Benassaya. Deezer currently has around 16 million active monthly users in more than 180 countries, including 6 million paying subscribers, and its catalog contains more than 40 million titles. The tagline on its website reads: «Deezer: where music lives.»

Fans make music their own

With new technologies, fans have not only discovered a new way to listen to music, they have also invented a new way to live music. Of course, they watch new videos, share them with their friends on social networks and comment on them. But above all, fans are making their favorite tunes their own by inventing new versions of them or even parodying them. Fans then pair these songs with images and post them on YouTube. This is undoubtedly a way for Millennials to emulate the stars they worship and pay tribute to their talents. But it is also a way for them to express their creativity using the technological means they now have at their disposal.

We've lost count of the number of remakes and parodies of «*Gangnam Style*», «*Harlem Shake*», «*Happy*» and «*Let It Go*». The latter hit is the theme song of the animated film Frozen, which was released in 2013. With box office receipts surpassing 1 billion dollars, it has become one of the most successful animated films of all time. For a few weeks after its release, its position in the box office rankings wavered before it settled into the top spot for several weeks in a row. One of the reasons that could explain the resurgence in interest for Frozen more than a month after it came out is the popularity of the song «*Let It Go*». So many fans posted covers of it on YouTube that Disney decided to authorize their outpouring of creativity and passion. Legions of young and not-so-young people have learned the lyrics and filmed themselves channeling Elsa, the film's heroine.

Initially a community of fans formed around this song, which went on to win an Oscar, and later around the film itself, which experienced a new surge in ticket sales. There are now more than 150,000 videos covering «*Let It Go*» on YouTube and the official video for the song, which is on the YouTube channel of Walt Disney Animation Studios, has garnered more than 550 million views.

Covering hit songs is also the specialty of Boyce Avenue, an American group that became famous on YouTube. In 2004, three brothers—Alejandro, Daniel and Fabian Manzano[1] – set out on a musical adventure. «*We've been playing music for a really long time. We started it as a hobby, as something fun we did for family and friends*», explains Fabian Manzano, the group's lead guitarist. «*We did it because we loved it and because all we wanted to do was play guitar and sing. We never thought that it would become a career. Actually, I went to school to be an architect and my older brother went to school to be a lawyer. We didn't know that music could be a real job. For us it was a dream. [...] In 2007, we posted our first video on YouTube and it started to do very well. Every day we got more and more views. And then, in 2008, we quit our day jobs to focus on Boyce Avenue 100%. Now we have more than 7 million subscribers on our YouTube channel. It's crazy!*»

Fabian, Alejandro and Daniel Manzano from the boys band "Boyce Avenue"

1 Interviewed by the authors in February 2015.

Link to Boyce Avenue's YouTube channel: https://www.youtube.com/user/boyceavenue

Their videos have now racked up nearly 3 billion views. In the description section of their channel, the band says: « *Because of your support we are the most viewed independent band in the world! We do what we love everyday because of you! Thanks so much!* » The group, which is very active on social media, also has a Facebook page with approximately 3 million likes and a Twitter account with more than 540,000 followers. Boyce Avenue like to interact with their fans. « *To be honest, it's kind of hard to find other artists on YouTube that tour as much as we do,* » explains Fabian Manzano. « *Touring is very hard and expensive, but it's one of our favorite parts of the job. We like to get out there and actually meet our fans face to face.* » The three musicians have already given many concerts all over the world. They have also founded their own label, 3 Peace Records. In the words of Fabian Manzano: « *We have more creative control this way. We can post any video we want, on whatever platform we want, and there is nothing or no one who can stand between us and our fans.* »

KEY TAKEAWAYS:

The music industry has been completely disrupted and its economic model is undergoing a full-on revolution. Free and easy access defines the new way in which fans listen to music. For those who get their music through streaming, the expectation is to have access at all times and everywhere to a colossal music library.

Music is listened to on multiple platforms. Fans discover songs and share them on YouTube and Facebook, and they listen to them on Spotify and Deezer. People download and listen to music on the go. The smartphone is today's Walkman. Music crosses borders phenomenally fast. Psy is a good example of an artist who would not have been as successful in the compartmentalized world of 20 years ago.

Fans interact with the latest hits and make them their own by creating new versions or remixing the original, the better to share them with others. Listening to and appreciating music is now a two-way street: it is a dual interaction between artists and their audience.

Chapter 6 – The movie and publishing industries are adapting to fans' tastes

« Michelle Phan has blazed a new path for women everywhere. Armed with passion, personality, business savvy and a YouTube account, she›s built a worldwide following from the ground up. Make Up : Your Life Guide to Beauty, Style, and Success – Online and Off shows how Michelle transformed her talent and creativity into a global brand. »

Robert Kyncl, Chief Business Officer, YouTube.

Once they led an anonymous existence behind their webcams. Then they became major personalities of the digital world. And now YouTube stars are conquering the «*real*», aka offline world. They are appearing on TV screens and the cover of magazines, and film-industry professionals are watching them closely. As YouTube stars land more and more roles in movies and television, they are transforming screens big and small. Their fans couldn't be happier.

YouTube stars: out to conquer TV and the silver screen

Norman Thavaud is one of the most famous comedian on the web in France. In 2011, he began posting short skits filmed in his bedroom to his YouTube channel, entitled «*Norman fait des vidéos*» («*Norman makes videos*»), which currently has more than 8 million subscribers. It wasn't long before he also ventured out on tour and landed his first movie role. In 2012, at the Grand Rex theater in Paris, he organized a show called Le Zapping Amazing (Amazing Channel Surfing) which brought together onstage a number of French web comedians, including Cyprien, Mister V, PV Nova, La Ferme Jérôme and others. In 2013, the second edition of the show toured throughout France. That same year, Norman Thavaud was featured in the movie Pas très normales activités (Not very normal activities), directed by Maurice Barthélémy. He has also starred in one-man shows, and is continuing to tour France.

Another example of Youtubers branching out into the movie industry is the 2014 comedy Camp Takota, directed by Nick and Chris Riedell. It showcases three e-stars: Grace Helbig, Hannah Hart and Mamrie Hart. This feature film was written by the latter, who hosts the popular show You Deserve a Drink on her own YouTube channel. These three real-life friends have a combined audience of 5.8 million subscribers to their respective channels and more than 560 million views. Camp Takota, which was initially distributed via the VHX digital distribution platform and also sold on iTunes for $9.99, was subsequently added to the Netflix catalog. The same crew released the movie sequel called "Dirty 30" in September 2016.

Grace Helbig, who has more than 3 million fans on YouTube, has also ventured into television, and in 2015, she began hosting her own show (The Grace Helbig Show) on the E! Entertainment network.

She is also the author of Grace's Guide: the Art of Pretending to Be a Grown-up, a New York Times #1 best-seller.

Trailer for Camp Takota:
https://www.youtube.com/watch?v=UVaBQuuwn7k

Fans: transforming the publishing industry

American author John Green is undoubtedly one of the world's most influential authors, and one of the most connected writers in the digital sphere. He has 5.2 million Twitter followers, and 3 million subscribers to Vlogbrothers, the YouTube channel he co-hosts with his brother, Hank Green. The channel boasts 650 million views, and since 2007 the brothers have been having a running conversation with each other via the videos they post to the platform. Their motto is « *Raising Nerdy to the Power of Awesome* ». The fan community that has sprung up around them is nicknamed Nerdfighters or Nerdfighteria.

Forbes magazine named John Green one of its top 100 celebrities of 2014 due to the resounding success of his book The Fault in Our Stars[1] and the film adaptation of the same name. He had already gained renown for his three previous novels: Looking for Alaska, An Abundance of Katherines[2] and Paper Towns[3].

First published in 2012, The Fault in Our Stars recounts the love story between two teenagers who have cancer. In 2014, the book was adapted as a feature film starring Shailene Woodley and Ansel Elgort. The movie, which had a budget of only 12 million dollars, earned more than $48 million at the box office in the US, which was quite a bit more than the $29 million earned by Edge of Tomorrow (also released that year), even though it starred Tom Cruise and had a budget of $175 million. The success of the film adaptation of The Fault in Our Stars mirrored that of the book. According to a Washington Post article published in June 2014, the novel sold more than 10.7 million copies, was translated into 46 languages, and spent 78 consecutive weeks on the New York Times list of best-selling young adult books.

The book and its film adaptation enjoyed their initial success on social networks. Nerdfighteria, the community of hyper-connected

1 John Green, The Fault in Our Stars (New York: Dutton, 2012).
2 John Green, An Abundance of Katherines (New York: Dutton, 2006).
3 John Green, Paper Towns (New York: Dutton, 2008).

fans of John Green and his brother, was primed to lend its support. According to a Variety article published in June 2014, the movie's trailer received more likes than any other preview in YouTube history, and fans sent out more than 1 million tweets about the film during the week it premiered in theaters. The acronym TFIOS (The Fault in Our Stars) also became a buzzword on social networks and even entered the vocabulary of young adults. Fans also shared countless photos of themselves with the book, or just pictures of its cover, which they posted on Instagram and other applications. An official Tumblr microblog with the name « *The Fault in Our Stars* » was even created so that fans could share photos about the movie, its actors, quotes from it, etc. More than just a book or movie, The Fault in Our Stars became a genuine social phenomenon that was created and sustained by social networks.

The film crew of "The Fault in Our Stars", from left to right, Josh Boone, Ansel Elgort, Shailene Woodley and John Green.

Link to the trailer for The Fault in Our Stars:
https://www.youtube.com/watch?v=9ItBvH5J6ss

Another book that took the world's social networks by storm was Girl Online, published in November 2014.[1] Written by Zoe Sugg, better known as Zoella, the novel tells the story of a teen girl whose blog becomes an overnight success. In its first week more than 78,000 copies were sold, making it the highest-selling first novel in the history of the United Kingdom—a record that until then had been held by J. K. Rowling, the author of the Harry Potter series.

Zoe Sugg, a 25-year-old Englishwoman, is a famous Youtuber, with nearly 11 million fans who eagerly follow the beauty, makeup and fashion tips she has been sharing since 2009. Her videos have garnered more than 830 million views and on Twitter she has more than 6.6 million followers. In short, just like her young public, Zoe Sugg is very connected. In fact, it was thanks to a 13-year-old fan of hers, who is the goddaughter of the CEO of Penguin Books, that she was able to establish contacts with the publishing house, which wagered that the book would be a huge hit and signed her to a contract.

A few days after her book came out, she posted the following message on her Twitter account: «*I'm legit blown away by this. I never in a million years thought that so many of you would pick up a copy of Girl Online. Almost wanna cry.*» However, a few weeks later, Zoella was accused of having used a ghostwriter for Girl Online. She took to Twitter in an attempt to defend herself: «*[...] for the doubters out there, of course I was going to have help from Penguin's editorial team in telling my story [...] Everyone needs help when they try something new*», she explained, adding that the story and characters were in fact her own creation.

This revelation was most disappointing for her fanbase, with whom she had established a relationship based on authenticity and sincerity. For several years, Zoella had revealed much about herself to her webfans, including her problems with panic attacks and anxiety. In fact, she had even become the digital ambassador of the Mind association, which launched the #DontPanicButton campaign in 2014. Consequently, this young vlogger will have to win back her fans' trust. She succeeded in doing so by writing the sequel, Girl Online: on tour all by herself.

Link to Zoella's YouTube channel trailer:
https://www.youtube.com/user/zoella280390

1 Zoe Sugg, Girl Online (New York: Penguin/Atria Books, 2014).

KEY TAKEAWAYS:

The movie and publishing industries are also connected to today's internet stars and are adapting to fans' tastes in order to better target the Millennial audience.

Using a computer or smartphone, becoming a YouTube star is within reach of anyone who is creatively gifted. It is now also possible to make the leap from the small to the big screen, and even to leverage one's online popularity to sell a book. Online stars are also becoming offline stars. Collaborations between brands and webstars is not limited to the digital sphere. In other words: Millennials can be reached beyond the internet.

Chapter 7 – Fans: revolutionizing the advertising industry

« YouTube creators are genius marketers. They understand concepts like how to do product placement and co-op marketing, how to build their own brands. There's a lot marketers can learn from them. »

Shiv Singh, Senior Vice-President of Global Brand and Marketing Transformation at Visa.

The internet cannot dissociate itself from advertising, which is its lifeblood. The e-economy could not exist without ads to finance it. A web in which fans feel endowed with a certain power, a certain strength, has repercussions for the advertising industry, which must adapt and evolve in order to stay attuned to consumers' desires and needs.

Advertising: out to conquer the digital realm

With the advent of new technologies, the advertising industry has been completely disrupted and has entered a new digital era. TV commercials now have to compete with online advertising, which keeps increasing its market share. Advertising Age, in an article published in October 2014, forecasted that, in 2016, spending on online advertising in the US would outstrip spending on TV advertising. It also reported that, according to a market study carried out by Forrester Research, spending on online advertising would reach nearly 103 billion dollars in 2019. For the next five years, the «*search*» segment, i.e., advertising and marketing via search engines, is expected to remain the primary beneficiary of advertising investments in the digital realm. The «*display*» segment, i.e., the purchasing of advertising space in the traditional sense, with integrated videos, banners, pull-down menus, etc., should follow closely on the heels of the search segment, while spending on social advertising—i.e., on social networks such as Facebook, Twitter, etc.—is expected to experience the strongest growth, with an increase of 18% according to Forrester Research.

When it comes to advertising on mobile devices, two players already capture nearly two-thirds of the market: Google and Facebook. According to Yannick Bolloré, CEO of Havas, a major French advertising firm: «*These two players are not exactly what we would call traditional advertising investments. In my view, what we are witnessing is the emergence of a new class of advertising investments which aim to fulfill another function. In terms of advertising, we don't communicate the same way on Google and Facebook as we do on TV or in print media. We have noted the emergence of new opportunities for brands to target their customers or prospects, whether via a search engine or a social network. We tend to think of advertising investments as [communicating vessels], but for me it's an allocation of resources that's evolving in a much more profound way than simply transferring budgets from one medium to another. The message itself is different.* »

While some may consider the advertising sales divisions of Google and Facebook to be adversarial competitors, others view them as serious partners. « *Perhaps the future will prove me wrong* », continues Yannick Bolloré, « *but I tend to foresee Google and Facebook being partners rather than competitors. I think they are becoming very important providers of advertising space for us. They are our number one international partners. We work hand in hand with them to propose customized communication solutions to our clients.* »

The advertising industry is experiencing rapid growth, driven primarily by the digital market. In an interview published in the Financial Times in December 2014, Maurice Lévy, the CEO of Publicis, a major French communication group, described the changes in the advertising industry as a « *digital tsunami* ». In order to confront this new paradigm and successfully meet the challenges arising from it, he says that at his company « *We employ geeks, techies and gamers.* » It's an approach that allows the needs and profiles of online consumers to be better understood. Last year, Publicis announced two acquisitions: Cybermedia, which provides web services to small and medium-sized enterprises in Belgium and the Netherlands, and Sapient, an American company in the digital communications industry. In so doing, the aim of Publicis is to stay on top of an ultra-competitive market and increase its international growth in digital communications following its failed merger in 2014 with American company Omnicom, the second largest firm in the industry.

In the same interview, Maurice Lévy reveals that « *Everyone is starting to worry about being "Ubered". [...] It's the idea that you suddenly wake up to find your legacy business gone... clients have never been so confused or concerned about their brands or their business model* ». The reference is to Uber, a taxi service that links drivers and riders directly via its mobile app. « *We employ geeks, techies and gamers. [...] Today advertising campaigns are so highly targeted that they are often not even seen by the general public* », explains Maurice Lévy in the same press article. Today, using cookies and various complex formulas, advertisers are capable of identifying the profile of people viewing content online and adjusting advertising to target them in near-real time. The idea is to aim well and hit the bull's-eye so that the marketing message is not lost in cyberspace.

The ever-more innovative content of advertising

«In this era of the skip-generation and multitasking it's much more complicated to capture people's attention than it once was», explains Yannick Bolloré, the CEO of Havas. *«It is critical to be much more impactful as soon as the ad is launched in order to get people's attention, and utilize the full potential of digital to create truly interactive ads. Authenticity is important in advertising. This generation is perfectly aware of what goes on behind the scenes and knows whether a brand has paid for an ad to target them [...]. Millennials are also keen on innovation. Content needs to be very innovative and incorporate this generation's badges of identity such as humor and self-deprecation. Millennials consume much more content than their elders, but not just any content. It has to interest them, be highly qualitative or meet a specific need that people share on social networks, related to the news, sports, humor, etc.»*

GoPro: both a producer and distributor of content

GoPro, a manufacturer of action cameras, regularly produces breathtaking films with magnificent images of the most extreme sports, shot in dramatic locations. These videos are generally posted on social networks. The brand doesn't just market to amateur athletes and sports enthusiasts, but also to the general public connected to new technologies. The promotional video produced for the release of the GoPro HERO3+ in 2013 has been viewed nearly 42 million times on YouTube. GoPro is both a creator of content by way of the videos the brand produces and a content distributor by way of its own YouTube channel, which boasts more than 4 million subscribers. Together with partner channels, GoPro videos have been viewed more than 1.4 billion times on YouTube.

GoPro has adopted a very innovative approach to communication by using social networks to target Millennials, who have turned away from traditional media, and therefore traditional ads.

Link to the «*GoPro Hero3*» video:
https://www.youtube.com/watch?v=A3PDXmYoF5U

The world of advertising has changed and so have its messages. People appreciate content creators who speak honestly, without deceit. According to Ted Wright, the CEO of Fizz, a marketing agency specializing in word-of-mouth marketing: «*It's all about going out and changing the way you're thinking and the two key changes are : you need to share instead of sell, you need to celebrate instead of tell.*»

Red Bull: event creator

Red Bull, producer of the world's top-selling energy drink, is not just a content creator but also an event creator. In October 2012, this Austrian brand sponsored the highest skydive on record. Parachutist Felix Baumgartner leapt, on camera, from nearly 24 miles (39 kilometers) above the Earth. This exploit was covered by the media throughout the world and watched live by more than 8 million people on YouTube. Since then, the video has been seen by nearly 40 million people on the web. Visibility doesn't get much better than that. No more need for commercials!

This is the highest-profile media event that Red Bull has pulled off, but the company has also lent its support to and showcased many other extreme sports such as car racing (Formula 1, etc.), surfing, snowboarding, and all variety of extreme jumping events (various kinds of diving, flying and jumping, freestyle motocross, etc.). The brand's number one aim is to surprise. The «*about*» page of its YouTube account, which has more than 5.5 million subscribers, reads: «*Experience the world of Red Bull like you have never seen it before.*» The videos posted on its channel have been viewed more than 1.5 billion times. By creating Red Bull Media House, its own media agency, the beverage brand turned the usual logic on its head. Now it is providing content to the traditional channels itself.

Link to the video «*Felix Baumgartner's supersonic freefall from 128k'*»:
https://www.youtube.com/watch?v=FHtvDA0W34I

The time it takes to promote something matters little now. On the web, creators don't hold back. The internet is free of the time constraints that limit most TV commercials to 30 seconds. On the web, ads can even run as long as five minutes—something that was unthinkable 30 years ago. These promotional videos are much more than just commercials: they are engaging and sometimes even encourage viewers to delve more deeply into the product itself. The ad for the Mercedes-Benz GLA-Class, which has an initial duration of 90 seconds, encourages viewers to get behind-the-scenes details and even outtakes from the making of the commercial in order to broaden what is now known as the « *user experience* ».

Mercedes-Benz and content in advertising

The advertisement for the Mercedes-Benz Class-GLA, which came out in 2013, imagines the new model being carved out of a monolith. Football players, a skateboarder, a dancing couple and even a deer pass by and sculpt an enormous black slab until it becomes the crossover SUV. The 90-second ad was designed to give viewers a glimpse into the universe of each character. The flagship video is backed by more than 25 hours of content, including an overview of the life of a deer in the forest. The video surprised advertising specialists and even web viewers with its audacity and creativity. It has been viewed on the web more than 5 million times. According to a case study carried out by Google, within a month of the release of this series of videos, the time all viewers combined spent watching them added up to nearly seven years.

Link to the Mercedes-Benz « *Monolith* » video:
https://www.youtube.com/watch? v=5SFf9nwrNds

According to Yannick Bolloré, « *Ads like Volvo's with Jean-Claude Van Damme or Evian's with the babies seem very innovative because they are shared on social media, but they are actually quite traditional and were created by traditional players in the advertising industry. What is revolutionary is how those ads were distributed. Some say that content is king and distribution is queen, but I think they are equally important and that you have to find a balance between them.* »

Volvo and viral advertising

In late 2013, Volvo came up with a novel ad featuring the actor Jean-Claude Van Damme. In this video, Van Damme, who is famous for his stunts and martial arts skills, stands on the side-view mirrors of two Volvo trucks as they roll backwards. Gradually, the gap between the semis increases as the actor, remaining completely still, descends into a full side split. The video has been viewed more than 80 million times and has spawned numerous parodies. The most famous of these features Chuck Norris wishing viewers «*Merry Christmas and Happy New Year*» as he descends into a split with his feet perched on the wings of two airplanes in flight, as 11 men balance on top of his head in a Christmas tree formation.

Link to the «*Volvo Trucks*» video:
https://www.youtube.com/watch?v=M7FIvfx5J10
Link to «*Chuck Norris – Parody Van Damme Volvo Commercial*»:
https://www.youtube.com/watch?v=dndHQzZPH0Q

What will be the future of digital advertising? Advertisers are already working on tailoring the message and creative content to each consumer, in real time. Currently, different ads can be shown depending on who is watching, but the actual content of a given video does not vary for different viewers. However, that is the direction in which advertisers are heading.

Brands target Millennials...

In an ad from December 2014 entitled «*Stop phubbing*[1] *around*», Coca-Cola chose to speak directly to Millennials. It even said as much in the disclaimer at the beginning of the video: «*THE FOLLOWING FILM CONTAINS LANGUAGE ONLY SUITABLE FOR PEOPLE WHO SPEND TOO MUCH TIME ONLINE.*» Its vocabulary is straight out of the digital lexicon: «*follow*», «*snap*», «*post*», «*tag*» and «*pin*», peppered with the occasional «*#*», «*like*» and «*comment*» to deliver the brand's message. Within a scant two months, the video was viewed more than 22 million times on YouTube.

Link to the «*Stop phubbing around*» video:
https://www.youtube.com/watch?v=8LLQIbr2-k0

1 Snubbing someone in favor of one's mobile phone.

... and make deals with YouTube stars

Certain brands are collaborating with web stars in order to have an even greater impact on Millennials. One example is mobile phone manufacturer LG, which chose Zach King, a YouTube and Vine star, for its LG G3 ad, which has been viewed more than 8 million times. It features the famous «*Viner*», known for his magic tricks, using the new LG smartphone to create even more magic.

Link to «*LG G3: Zach King*»:
https://www.youtube.com/watch?v=bRE08hkXvfU

Another brand, another YouTube star: since 2013, Coca-Cola has featured the artist Kurt Hugo Schneider and his famous associate, Sam Tsui, in a number of surprising ads. Both stars combined are followed by more than 10 million subscribers on YouTube. They include few or no instruments, but many Coke bottles, and cover hit songs such as «*Safe and Sound*» by Capital Cities and «*Feel So Close*» by Calvin Harris.

Link to the video for «*I Feel So Close*», covered by Sam Tsui, featuring Kurt Schneider:
https://www.youtube.com/watch?v=7iGdMeaelas

For several years now, brands have been taking an interest in YouTube stars—not only because they are famous (their fans number in the millions worldwide) but also because of the influence they have on their community of fans, for whom they are genuine opinion leaders. Web stars who wear a certain article of clothing or use a given beauty product and make that known over social networks have fans who follow and listen to them. Marketing professionals also seek to reach fans who will be just as engaged and loyal to those brands as they are to the stars they idolize.

Aéropostale, an American clothing brand specializing in apparel for children and teenagers, has established a partnership with Bethany Mota, who is followed by more than 10 million subscribers on YouTube and has more than 5 million followers on Instagram, where she posts pictures of her clothes. In fact, this 20-year-old fashionista has more followers on Instagram than all the major fashion magazines combined. The influence of this web star on her young trend-spotting fans can hardly be overstated. This new icon of off-the-rack fashion has also collaborated on ad campaigns with other clothing brands such as JCPenney and Forever 21. But with Aéropostale, Bethany Mota has realized one of her dreams: designing her own line of clothes and jewelry.

YouTube star, Bethany Mota taking a selfie with a young fan in a Aéropostale's store in Toronto in 2013.

Link to Bethany Mota's YouTube channel:
https://www.youtube.com/user/Macbarbie07

KEY POINTS:

The world of advertising must become more and more innovative to target Millennials, who hungry for new and original content. Advertising messages must be authentic and not try to deceive the consumer. Brands can even become event creators—as is the case with Red Bull—in order to contribute content, communicate with their customer base and win over new fans. They also recruit the stars of the web in order to speak the same language as Millennials.

Chapter 8 – Fans are gamers

« We turned a 'terrible idea' into a $970 million company. »

Justin Kan, founder of the video-game streaming site Twitch, at TechCrunch Disrupt London, October 2014.

More than a passion, a pastime or a distraction, video games have become a veritable «*e-sport*» for fans connected to their consoles and all variety of joysticks. The phenomenon is global. In 2014 there were some 1.8 billion gamers, i.e., nearly a quarter of the world's population, according to a market study carried out by Newzoo in June of that year and published on the VentureBeat website, which specializes in tech news. The stereotype of gamers as young male geeks is outdated. Women have also joined the world of video games and now represent nearly half of all gamers according to an article published in the Wall Street Journal in August 2014.

The gaming industry has become so colossal it is now the number one entertainment industry in the world. According to a study carried out in May 2014 by Newzoo, an agency specializing in market studies in video game industry, the industry is forecasted to exceed $100 billion in revenue in 2017. Fans are faithful to the games they love. They swap tips with other gamers and challenge each other. They scan the forums and closely monitor news about new games.

Fans of online games

The games that fans enjoy the most are online and involve multiple players. They are known as massively multiplayer online games (MMOG) and they are the very essence of e-sports. Thanks to MMOGs and MMORPGs (massively multiplayer online role-playing games), gaming has taken on a social dimension by linking gamers who do not know one another or even live in the same country but who, once online, are ready to play their favorite game together. Among these video games, League of Legends and World of Warcraft (WoW) are hugely successful worldwide. Currently over 100 million people play League of Legends every month, according to figures released by the publisher Riot Games. As for World of Warcraft, it's an online role-playing game developed by Blizzard Entertainment 10 years ago and passed the threshold of 10 million registered players in 2014. Its fans have even created an online encyclopedia for it: WikiWoW.

Another hugely successful video game is Minecraft. Launched in 2009, this construction game has a large fan community. More than 12 million people have already liked the game's Facebook page and there are many forums dedicated to it. To date, more than 23 million people have bought a PC or Mac version of Minecraft according to the game's official website.

The appearance of new video-game streaming sites such as Twitch, as well as the development of YouTube channels dedicated to gaming, having transformed this e-sport into a spectator sport. Fans are no longer just players of video games, they have also become spectators of them. It's a new trend that has surfaced: more and more enthusiasts are watching online video games played by others who, in addition to deftly controlling their consoles, share a running commentary on the action. This is undoubtedly what is enjoyed by their online spectators, who now watch online video game matches as if they were watching a football game.

The Video Games Championship "League of Legends" in 2014 in California.

Twitch: the social network of gamers

Faced with the growing success of his streaming video game channel, Justin Kan launched Twitch in 2011. The platform, which allows one to watch video game matches on demand or live, also lets web viewers comment on the players' actions in real time, chat with the global audience online, and appreciate the talents of these e-sports experts. It's a real plus for fans!

Twitch is the favored social network of gamers. A full-fledged, tight-knit community has sprung up consisting of gamers who share their videos, spectators who interactively watch them play, and video game publishers who now have a direct relationship with the fans of their games.

According to Twitch, every month more than 100 million people surf the platform and interact with more than 2 million live-streaming users. In 2014, Twitch generated the fourth-highest level of traffic in the United States, after Netflix, Google and Apple, and it was bought by Amazon for nearly 1 billion dollars.

In September 2015, Twitch organized its first-ever TwitchCon. Held in San Francisco, the convention is akin to the annual VidCon event that brings together YouTube stars and their fans. «*Twitch broadcasters have the most passionate fans, so we want to create an amazing experience where they can come together in person*», explains Emmett Shear, the chairman and CEO of Twitch, on the company's official blog. «*TwitchCon will be an opportunity for the entire community—broadcasters, game developers, viewers, and us—to play and learn together.*»

PewDiePie, YouTube's biggest star

With more than 49 million subscribers and approximately 13 billion views, PewDiePie hosts the most-watched channel on YouTube. His real name is Felix Kjellberg and since 2010 he has been making videos of himself testing and commenting on video games. The 27-year-old Swede is fond of grimaces, shouts, insults and especially montages, which give his videos a personal flair. In 2013, he uploaded a compilation of his favorite moments, which has been viewed more than 68 million times. In June 2014, he revealed to the Wall Street Journal that he earned more than $4 million a year, primarily from the advertising shown before his videos.

Link to PewDiePie's YouTube channel:
https://www.youtube.com/results? search_query=pewdiepie

KEY TAKEAWAYS:

Gaming brings together a whole community of fans. The entire video game industry is globalized and connected.

Chapter 9 – Fans are becoming journalists

« What we found was that Generation Y is absolutely consumed with news. They love news, it's one of their biggest passion points. The problem is they've been disenfranchised by traditional media outlets and because of that—look, if the world was going along tickety-boo and the Fourth Estate was doing its job, VICE would not be purveying news. »

Shane Smith,
co-founder of Vice, at TechCrunch Disrupt, May 2014.

Social networks are more than just platforms for socializing; with time, they have also taken on a new function: informing.

New forms of news media have emerged

Between December 2010 and January 2011, Facebook, Twitter and YouTube began taking on the role of news media during the revolutions in Tunisia, Egypt, Libya, Yemen, Syria and Bahrain. As early as 2009, these social platforms enabled Iranians to inform the world about and share images of the demonstrations that followed the re-election of president Mahmoud Ahmadinejad. One year later, the web and smartphone applications became genuine communication tools that played a central role during the Arab Spring.

The events that rocked this part of the globe starting in late 2010 have sometimes even been called the "Facebook revolution" or the "Twitter revolution" because these social networks allowed demonstrators to organize, mobilize, get news and share news with others, alert foreign media, and even rally protesters. Facebook, Twitter and YouTube allowed people to report directly from the uprisings, and to a certain extent they even precipitated, accelerated and amplified them. At the time, Alec Ross, who was Hillary Clinton's Senior Advisor for Innovation at the State Department, called the internet the "Che Guevara of the 21st century".

Social networks and the ‹net gave rise to and fed the Arab protest movement, which transformed into intense demonstrations. Facebook, Twitter and YouTube focused the world's attention on these events, which led to the fall of regimes that had been in place for decades in Tunisia, Egypt and Libya. Bloggers and other influencers on the web also provided information to the traditional foreign media. However, some political scientists have stated that the role of the internet in the Arab Spring was exaggerated by the traditional media, and that the demonstrations that quickly spread throughout the Arab world were first and foremost street demonstrations that were led by men and women demanding political, social and societal change.

Be that as it may, the population did in fact use social networks during this period to express its discontent loudly and clearly. According to a study published in 2012 by the European Institute of the Mediterranean, entitled Social Media in the Arab World: the Impact on Youth, Women and Social Change, the use of Facebook and Twitter increased dramatically in the Arab world during 2011. The source cited by the study was a series of reports produced by the Arab Social Media Report. The number of Facebook users in the region nearly doubled between December 2010 and December 2011, going from more than 21 million profiles to around 38 million. The number of tweets published in the Arab world in September 2011 was estimated to be 36 million, i.e., more than 1 million tweets per day. During the course of the same month, the most popular hashtags in Arab countries were #bahrain, #egypt, #syria, #kuwait, etc.

One of the emblematic figures of the Egyptian revolution is Wael Ghonim. In addition to being Head of Marketing of Google Middle East and North Africa, he was also the anonymous administrator of the Facebook page "We are all Khaled Said", created following the death of Mr. Said (sometimes spelled Saeed), a 28-year-old blogger who was beaten to death by the police in Egypt in June 2010. The page enjoys widespread support among the Egyptian Facebook community.

On January 14, 2011, Wael Ghonim used Facebook to issue a call to protest on the 25th of that month. Via the Internet, other organizations also called for a "day of rage". That date is now considered to be the first day of the Egyptian revolution. However, on the 27th, Ghonim was arrested and held for 12 days. Upon his release on February 7, he was moved to discover the scale of both the protests and the number of victims. During a televised interview with Ghonim, which was broadcast on Dream TV, his tears moved the Egyptian public, which finally put a name and face to this originator of the uprising. On February 11, President Hosni Mubarak, in power since 1981, resigned under the pressure of the protests.

In an attempt to tamp down the protest movement, the Egyptian and Libyan authorities even attempted to shut down the internet, which they succeeded in doing for periods of several hours to several days. However, that did not stop Egyptians from uploading a huge number of videos to YouTube during the two most intense weeks of popular action. So it was that social networks made their debut in the news media world, sometimes competing with but more often complementing traditional media.

In 2012, a very different type of event brought social networks even further to the fore. In October of that year, Hurricane Sandy hit the East

Coast of the United States. In many locations, landline telephone and cable internet service were cut off due to flooding and violent winds. More than 8 million homes found themselves without electricity. Mobile phones became an indispensable tool to stay informed and safe, and to help those in need. The authorities in New York and New Jersey, the two states hit hardest by the hurricane, used social networks such as Twitter to communicate a great deal of practical information to the public, including the trajectory of the hurricane, safety advice, emergency numbers, road closures, the status of the electrical and telephone networks, etc. According to Twitter, between October 27 and November 1, more than 20 million tweets were sent with the hashtags "Sandy" and "hurricane". According to the digital media website Mashable, more than 1.3 million photos of the storm were posted on Instagram. The most impressive images were even disseminated by the press agencies.

Hence, social networks are becoming a source of information, a full-fledged medium, and even a portal in which content is showcased. The internet media company BuzzFeed has understood better than others how to produce, communicate and disseminate information in the era of social networks. Created in 2006 by Jonah Peretti, who was also a founder of The Huffington Post, BuzzFeed has more than 200 million unique visitors per month. In a 2014 interview with InaGlobal.fr, Scott Lamb, the vice-president of BuzzFeed International, said "The key measurement for us isn't just the audience, it's the sharing. Social networks are our front page. Our readers don't visit the home pages of websites, they go onto social networks to find out what's going on in the world, so that's where BuzzFeed's stories have to be." According to Google Analytics, about 75% of BuzzFeed's audience comes from social networks. The company also intends to go into investigative journalism in order to diversify its content, which until now has been mostly light entertainment.

YouTube is becoming a news channel

YouTube has also become a world-class platform for traditional news media channels that have opted to create their own YouTube channel to make their content available to all. Euronews is a pioneer in the field, having launched itself on the video-sharing site back in 2007. Euronews reached a record 13.6 million unique viewers during the month of December 2013.[1] It now has 20 YouTube channels, including seven themed channels with a large number of subscribers, and is increasing its audience.

Today, practically every TV station has its own YouTube channel. For traditional media outlets, what's important is juggling between their TV broadcasts, their YouTube channel(s), their website, their mobile app and the various social networks in order to increase their visibility, their standing and, ultimately, their audience and advertising revenue. At the same time, other news channels have gotten their start on YouTube, such as VICE and The Young Turks. Their target audience is Millennials and their credo is authenticity in reporting.

Shane Smith has become a tycoon of contemporary media. In 1994 he co-founded the urban magazine The Voice of Montreal. Two years later it became VICE. Now he heads the Vice Media empire, worth more than 2.5 billion dollars. In 2005, he launched the VICE YouTube channel, which now has more than 7 million subscribers. Its specialty: "exploring uncomfortable truths". In late 2013, the Vice News channel also appeared on YouTube. Its tagline is "an international news channel created by and for a connected generation".[2] Vice News, which has more than 2 million YouTube subscribers, specializes in investigative and even undercover journalism. Its original documentaries have a fairly provocative tone and are meant to be «*unfiltered*».

Shane Smith, Co-Founder & CEO of Vice at Techcrunch Disrupt in New York in 2014.

1 Euronews, February 2014.
2 The Vice News channel on YouTube.

Links to the Vice and Vice News channels on YouTube :
https://www.youtube.com/user/vice
https://www.youtube.com/user/vicenews

Vice News came into the limelight in 2014 with its 42-minute-long report on the Islamic State, which was viewed by more than 7 million people on the internet. The network also covered the conflict in Ukraine. When Vice News was launched, Shane Smith told *Fortune* magazine: *"[Traditional media people are] saying we're not news, and we're saying we are, but we don't really care what they're calling us anymore because of our audience. None of Generation Y is watching TV or watching the news. There's no battle, there's no fight. You lost. You guys have the boomers and we have Gen Y."*

Vice Media has a presence in more than 80 countries and currently has about a dozen YouTube channels covering a wide range of topics, including news, sports, music, technology and cooking, among others. In an article published in French magazine *Télérama* in October 2014, Shane Smith notes that « *Vice was considered to be a niche media outlet because Gen Y was considered to be niche. Now that's it's taking over, we're becoming generalists. People are surprised that we've gone from trivial crap to Ebola. But we're growing up along with our audience. If we didn't change, it would be a problem."* Smith has never stopped trumpeting his ambition: *"I'm not going to be the next CNN, I'm not going to be the next ESPN, I'm not going to be the next MTV... I'm going to be CNN times 10, ESPN times 10 and MTV times 10.»*

Fans: new journalists, new citizen journalists

Whether they're 'net surfers, webcammers, vloggers or Youtubers, fans are producing video content on YouTube, reporting and commenting on events via Facebook and Twitter, being amateur photojournalists on Instagram and Snapchat, etc. In short, fans are becoming journalists—citizen journalists, in a manner of speaking. In this connected and participative world where everyone can film and be a witness to an event, the practice of amateur journalism has evolved and spread. Even new types of press agencies have emerged. Created in 2010, Storyful is the first social network-based press agency to sell verified and authenticated "user content" to editorial offices throughout the world, including to the New York Times, the Wall Street Journal, ABC, BBC and France 24, among others. Storyful is often described as a 21st-century press agency and, as such, it is competing with traditional agencies such as Reuters or AP. Thanks to cutting-edge technology and a wide network of contacts, Storyful's journalists have been successful at identifying newsworthy information, photos and videos posted to social networks, including Twitter, Instagram, YouTube and Facebook. Using this approach, it was the first agency to break the story of the Boston Marathon bombing in 2013. Founded by Irish journalist Mark Little in 2010, Storyful was bought by Rupert Murdoch's News Corp for 25 million dollars in 2013.

For Michael Peters,[1] CEO of the Euronews television channel, *"Fans are journalists and much more. They are the media. Fans are the true media of tomorrow. There is a shift in power. As a media company, we are just a tool, a medium that allows fans to arrive at their own opinions. They consume a lot of news but are poorly informed, so for us the goal is to try to ensure that they are well informed. The future, in this relationship with fans, is to try to inform them well, but not necessarily about everything or all the time."*

Link to the Euronews channel on YouTube :
https://www.youtube.com/user/euronewsfr

KEY TAKEAWAYS :

Social networks are the new media, and fans are citizen journalists who report news and share it in real time. Interaction and authenticity must be the keywords of today's news industry.

The traditional media no longer have a monopoly on the news. Video platforms and social networks, which are both numerous and fragmented, are the primary sources of information for Millennials. The latter seek information that is authentic and unfiltered. Vice News, a "digital native" channel, represents serious competition for traditional news channels. Moreover, thanks to cameras (including action cameras) and the new platforms, those users who are both mobile and active can make a name for themselves as reporters, and even position themselves to challenge the traditional media.

1 Interviewed by the authors in December 2014.

Chapter 10 – When celebrities are funded by fans

«I think people have been obsessed with the wrong question, which is, 'How do we make people pay for music?' What if we started asking, 'How do we let people pay for music?».

Musician Amanda Palmer, speaking at a TED Talk entitled «The Art of Asking», March 2013.

Crowdfunding is undoubtedly one of the most tangible demonstrations of the power of fans, who fund what they like and like what they fund. Stars turn to their fans to develop new projects. And even unknowns with good ideas are giving crowdfunding a go, bypassing bank financing in favor of the visibility of the 'net.

Crowdfunding allows anyone—entrepreneurs, content creators, artists, scientists and even associations—to raise funds online to finance a project. This is funding in which the go-between has been removed from the equation, and is made possible by the internet and the development of social networks. Crowdfunding creates a direct relationship between the project initiator and funders prepared to back the project. Funds are provided, in the form of a donation or a loan, in exchange for something in return—often an in-kind reward or equity in the start-up's capital. For each funding campaign, which is limited in duration, the entrepreneur must post an explanation to potential backers of the project's goals, and set a fundraising target to ensure the project's viability. If the amount is reached by the campaign's fundraising deadline, the project is funded. If it is not, the funds are returned to the investors.

The crowdfunding industry is growing rapidly. An article published in Forbes magazine in August 2014 refers to a report issued by Massolution, a consulting company specializing in the industry, according to which $2.7 billion was raised through crowdfunding in 2012 and $5.1 billion was raised in 2013.

Out of the many sites offering this service, there are two that stand out: Kickstarter and Indiegogo. Kickstarter, founded in New York in 2009, has already enabled more than 115,000 projects to be funded thanks to 12 million backers who collectively raised more than 2.7 billion dollars. Indiegogo, launched one year earlier in California, has experienced a 1,000% increase in funds raised over the past two years.

One of the most successful campaigns has been Amanda Palmer's. In 2012, the American singer raised more than $1.2 million thanks to 25,000 generous donors, all of whom are fans of her music and were prepared to fund the release of her upcoming album. She did not expect such a large amount, having aimed for $100,000. She currently has more than 1 million followers on Twitter and has often used the site to ask her fans for help, e.g.: a roof to sleep under while on tour, a piano to borrow for a few songs, and so forth. During a TED Talk she gave in February 2013, Palmer explained the reasons for the success of her campaign launched on Kickstarter several months earlier. On stage, before a prestigious audience, the young artist theorized about «*the art of asking*»: «*And the media asked, 'Amanda, the music business is tanking and you encourage piracy. How did you make all these people pay for music?' And the real answer is, I didn't make them. I asked them. And through the very act of asking people, I'd connected with them, and when you connect with them, people want to help you.*» Before she made her living as a singer, Amanda Palmer was a «*living statue*»: she would don a wedding dress and perch motionless on top of a box on the sidewalk. That's where she gained her experience in «*the art of asking*»: «*My music career has been spent trying to encounter people on the internet the way I could on the box. So blogging and tweeting not just about my tour dates and my new video but about our work and our art and our fears and our hangovers, our mistakes... and we see each other. And I think when we really see each other, we want to help each other. I think people have been obsessed with the wrong question, which is, 'How do we make people pay for music?' What if we started asking, 'How do we let people pay for music?'*»

Her vision of music is revolutionary.

The American music artist, Amanda Palmer on stage in 2013.

Link to the video «*Amanda Palmer: The art of asking*»: https://www.youtube.com/watch? v=xMj_P_6H69g

Crowdfunding exists in every field now: movies, music, sports, publishing, video games, scientific research, start-up launches, etc. In short, fans have wide-reaching interests and are especially fond of projects that are innovative and genuine.

Freddie Wong is both a filmmaker and an actor. He specializes in special effects and runs his own YouTube channel, called RocketJump, which has racked up some 1.3 billion views and 7.7 million subscribers. In 2012, he launched a web series on the channel called «*Video Game High School*» (VGHS), combining action and comedy. To finance it, he launched a fundraiser on Kickstarter. Together with his team, he managed to raise more than $270,000 for season 1 and more than $800,000 for season 2. In 2014, Freddie Wong announced a new fundraising campaign, this time on the competing crowdfunding site, Indiegogo, which offered more flexibility by allowing PayPal to be used for online payments. He received nearly $900,000 for season 3. The web series is a huge success, with an audience that has viewed it more than 110 million times on YouTube. Clearly, the fans are eager to fund it.

Link to the RocketJump channel on YouTube:
https://www.youtube.com/user/freddiew

KEY TAKEAWAYS:

Crowdfunding is a new industry that emerged thanks to new technologies and fans' buy-in and participation. It is based on a genuine relationship between the two parties involved: those who venture out in search of direct funding and those who believe in a new project they would like to see come to fruition. The funds raised come in from around the world.

Chapter 11 – Fans: champions for a cause

«Look at the amazing positive impact you bros have made!! Thank you!! @charitywater»

«weet sent by YouTube star Felix Kjellberg, aka PewDiePie, after launching a charity campaign for the association Charity: Water (https://twitter.com/charitywater), through which more than $440,000 was raised.

«Way to go for saving Gotham!»

President Barack Obama, in a message of support for «Batkid», posted to Vine

In addition to being active on social networks, fans are politically committed. They support a cause and let the whole world know about it. They like the Facebook pages of associations they care about, and tweet or retweet messages of support. They mobilize for a cause and sometimes put in some hard work for it.

A campaign gone viral

Launched in June 2014 on social networks, the Ice Bucket Challenge is a campaign supporting the fight against amyotrophic lateral sclerosis (ALS), also known as Lou Gehrig's disease, a little known degenerative nerve disorder. The challenge, for those who accept it, is to be filmed having a bucket of ice water poured over one's head, then challenge three other people to do the same within the next 24 hours. Anyone who declines the challenge is supposed to make a donation to the ALS Association. It is not unusual for participants who pour the ice bucket over their heads to also give money. The video is then generally posted on Facebook. More than 17 million such videos were posted to the site between June 1 and September 1, 2014. According to the social network, these videos have been viewed by more than 440 million people a total of more than 10 billion times.

But how did the Ice Bucket Challenge go viral, spreading around the world in a few weeks and inspiring the participation of celebrities as diverse as Cristiano Ronaldo, Justin Bieber, George W. Bush and Tom Cruise? It was an American athlete, Pete Frates, who is afflicted by Lou Gehrig's disease himself, who made the challenge famous. The former baseball player, who can no longer walk or talk, posted the challenge on his Facebook page with the assistance of Rob Van Winckle, better known by the name Vanilla Ice. At first it was Frates's Boston friends who took the challenge, followed by local authorities and politicians in the region. It then spread via the web and was taken by the CEO of Facebook, Mark Zuckerberg, who in turn challenged Bill Gates, the billionaire cofounder of Microsoft, who also accepted it. So it was that the challenge went global. According to Facebook, the 10 countries that were the most involved were the United States, Australia, New Zealand, Canada, Mexico, Brazil, Germany, the Philippines, India and Puerto Rico. Both celebrities and unknowns have taken the challenge and challenged others—not just to spread awareness of Lou Gehrig's disease, but also to have fun or polish their image on the social networks. Whatever their reasons, the campaign has gotten results, having raised more than $100 million for the ALS

Association, compared to the $3 million dollars raised the preceding year.

Link to the « *Bill Gates ALS Ice Bucket Challenge* » video: https://www.youtube.com/watch?v=XS6ysDFTbLU

So do social networks have a heart? You'd certainly think so after hearing the story of Miles Scott, a 5-year-old with leukemia who became a superhero for a day in San Francisco. The Make-a-Wish Foundation helps fulfill the wishes of children with life-threatening medical conditions. In November 2003, thanks to foundation, Miles, aka Batkid, donned a cape and black mask to save his city from the bad guys. San Francisco itself was transformed into « *Gotham City* » and thousands of people, including the police and local authorities, helped Miles fulfill his dream before a supportive crowd of more than 20,000, a sight that was quite moving for many of them. His story was widely circulated via the web and social networks. According to information provided on the website of the ALS Foundation, nearly 16,000 photos were shared on Instagram and more than 555,000 tweets with the hashtags #batkid or #SFBatkid were posted, about 13% of which originated from outside of the US. The topic was also posted about in more than 117 countries, especially in Canada, the United Kingdom and Australia. Even President Obama sent Batkid a message of support via a video posted on Vine.

Miles Scott is a 5-year old kid suffering from Leukemia who made his dream come true by becoming Bat Kid, a superhero for a day in San Francisco.

Link to the « *Official Batkid Video* »:
https://www.youtube.com/watch? v=Gw3aWPxtpfE

From « I am Neda » to « #JeSuisCharlie »

Social networks also serve to rally people, to call for national or even international unity, and to defend a cause, a right or a freedom. In 2009, a 26-year-old Iranian, Neda Agha-Soltan, was killed by a bullet while she was on the sidelines of a demonstration organized to protest the reelection of Mahmoud Ahmadinejad. A 40-second amateur video showing her dying, then dead, was uploaded to social networks and within a few hours had been seen throughout the world. She had unwittingly become an icon of the insurrection, the face of the Iranian Green Movement. Thousands of people viewed the video, wrote poems, posted message of support and created Facebook pages in her memory with the hashtag « *#neda* ». Many videos with the leitmotiv « *I am Neda* » have made the rounds of the web, making

this young woman a symbol of the values of peace, freedom and democracy.
A few years later, it was the hashtag «*#JeSuisCharlie*» that spread around the world in just a few hours. In the aftermath of the terrorist attack of January 7, 2015 against the staff of French newspaper Charlie Hebdo, during which 12 people died, the artistic director of Stylist magazine expressed his emotion by publishing a banner on his Twitter profile with three words on it: «*Je suis Charlie*» in white and gray against a black background. Within the space of three days, the message was retweeted more than 5 million times. Demonstrating both the strong emotions stirred throughout the world by these tragic events and the universality of the message, «*#JeSuisCharlie*» was also translated into many languages, giving us «*#IAmCharlie*», «*#YoSoyCharlie*», «*#IchBinCharlie*», etc.

Joachim Roncin[1], who penned the phrase, remains impressed by the degree to which it resonated. «*I wrote a message that was personal, spontaneous, that concerned me directly, that expressed something I felt at that moment, and then the social networks took care of the rest*», he explains. «*Never for a second did I imagine that the slogan would in any way go viral*», he notes, adding that «*If people identified with this message, it's because it's a sincere message and I think that any sincere message succeeds in some way; if the message is too calculated, too studied, too well-thought-out, it won't work.*» They are three words that, according to Roncin, defend «*freedom of the press, freedom of speech and the fact of not being afraid. It goes beyond Charlie Hebdo.*»

For Joachim Roncin, part of the success of the phrase is that it is a «*360-degree message that speaks to everyone and to all religions; it is nonpartisan, completely apolitical; it is a message of support*». Within just a few hours, Roncin, who only had 400 followers on Twitter before the tragedy, saw his message appear as the Facebook profile picture of people everywhere. Now more than 7,500 people follow his tweets. «*It was a giddy feeling*», he says. Joachim Roncin is now something of an opinion leader, an «*influencer*» on social networks. «*I didn't express myself much on Twitter before, but now I'm even more careful about what I post, because in spite of myself I've become the spokesman of a noble cause. [...] I created a message; the phenomenon then created itself on the social networks*», he notes,

1 Interviewed by the authors in February 2015.

adding that he has felt a bit as though his words have been taken away from him.

Roncin holds doubts, however, about the role that social networks can play as a tool to defend a cause. « *People told themselves: 'I'm posting this message because I'm showing my solidarity.' But after that, the idea of supporting a cause, of being proactive... I don't really know whether that can work on social networks because there are many causes to support. So I doubt there can be a real impact via the social networks* », he explains, before concluding that « *ultimately people are mostly just conduits on the social networks.* »

Whether they are just conduits or are passionate activists, fans use social networks to make their voices heard, to support a cause or to show their solidarity. Often, this lasts no longer than a single campaign. But regardless of fans' degree of involvement or the genuineness of their commitment, ultimately it is the aim of mobilization that triumphs, through the encouragement and publicity provided by those very fans.

KEY TAKEAWAYS:

On social networks, fans are becoming spokespersons and conduits for causes they support.
In our hyperconnected, globalized world, the viral nature of the movements supported online contributes in a real way to media campaigns.

Chapter 12 – Fans take an interest in politics

« Your voice is more powerful than that of the President of the United States. »

Barack Obama, speaking to YouTube star Bethany Mota about preventing cyberbullying, during an interview with three Youtubers in January 2015,

Politicians all over the world go on social networks to communicate directly and immediately with activists, voters and citizens, without any intermediaries. This makes them much more accessible by allowing them to engage in a more dynamic and appealing conversation with the public.

Political leaders juggle multiple social network accounts, including Facebook and YouTube, but it is undoubtedly Twitter that enjoys their greatest favor. Its short format—only 140 characters—enables users to send messages quickly and easily while keeping them focused and incisive. Politicians have been using the site to express themselves in a freer, more personal way, which has made their tweets an important source of information for journalists. Social networks also provide political figures with a means to sidestep the traditional media. Twitter is a social platform where political leaders reveal their thoughts and promote themselves, and even showcase themselves or make revelations. The flip side is that it is also where they tend to make the most gaffes and blunders.

In 2016, the five political figures who were the most followed on Twitter were: Barack Obama, with more than 80 million followers; Pope Francis who, with his nine accounts in different languages, has more than 29 million followers; the prime minister of India, Narendra Modi, who with more than 25 million followers is the most followed politician in Asia; the president of Indonesia, Susilo Bamban Yudhoyono; and President of Turkey, Recep Erdogan (9.4 million followers respectively)

President Obama has said that digital technology and social networks represent a major challenge. During his runs for office, he has surrounded himself with a large team who have supported his communications on social networks. One of the challenges of the White House has been to increase the president's popularity among young people. What better what to do that than by communicating on the video channels they watch the most, and by speaking with the stars they idolize? That was precisely why three YouTube celebrities interviewed Barack Obama in January 2015. GloZell Green, who is well known for her comedy and her colorful lipstick; Bethany Mota, the 21-year-old fashion maven; and science and technology geek Hank Green (brother of John Green), questioned the US president about various topics a few days after his State of the Union speech before Congress. Together, the three have more than 17 million subscribers on YouTube. The impact that the interview could have on social networks was therefore clear. The video has been viewed more than 3 million times on the White House YouTube channel, and the hashtag #YouTubeAsksObama inspired a large number of questions and comments. At the end of the interview, the president made a point of saying: «*I'm so proud of what you guys are doing because—this is the power of, [you] know, what the internet's all about. You know, you can create content, and there's not all these barriers to entry and suddenly you know, you get millions of people who are listening to you and in a conversation with you. And it's a great treat for me because, you know, more and more, there are audiences that get turned off by the traditional, you know, news shows or the traditional debates, and so for me to be able to reach your audiences and just hopefully give them a sense of that what we do here in Washington, what government does, actually matters and makes a difference in their lives.*»

YouTube video of Barack Obama's weekly address

Link to «*The YouTube interview with President Obama*»: https://www.youtube.com/watch?v=GbR6iQ62v9k

Political figures also use social networks to send strong messages. The uniqueness of the medium can encourage users to share novel ideas. Queen Rania of Jordan, who has a very large Twitter following, has had her own YouTube channel since 2007. Her videos there have been viewed a total of more than 14 million times. One of the videos she has uploaded is entitled «*Send me your stereotypes*». In it, she invites viewers to send her their questions about the Arab world so that clichés about the Middle East can be dispelled. In her launch video from 2008, she says: «*I want people to know the real Arab world, to see it unedited, unscripted and unfiltered.*»

Link to the video «*Send me your stereotypes*»:
https://www.youtube.com/watch? v=TFf897bUW2Y

Political figures also post symbolic messages to social networks. In 2007, Queen Elizabeth II was the first monarch to start a YouTube channel, which was launched on the 50th anniversary of her first televised address.

On «*The British Monarchy*» channel, videos about the charity activities of the royal family are posted regularly. Even though the channel has only 157 000 subscribers, its videos have been viewed more than 48 million times. The Queen even came in person to Google's offices in London to create a YouTube video with the assistance of the site's founder, Chad Hurley.

Link to the video «*The Queen visits Google London*»:
https://www.youtube.com/watch? v=8xDTZMYfa6g

KEY TAKEAWAYS:

There are no longer as many barriers between political leaders and online activists. They now communicate directly via social networks, without filters or intermediaries. Politicians can no longer do without social platforms, which represent a real plus for their communication strategies. At the same, time it has become easier to call out those politicians who attempt to deceive their audience, which expects clear and honest messages from them.

Chapter 13 – Fans and their love for sports

« We are reaching and engaging a huge demographic of 'digital natives', who have very different sports media consumption patterns and requirements. »

John West, Founder and CEO of the Whistle Sports
multi-channel network
January 2015.

Between the Winter Olympics in Sochi and the World Cup in Brazil, 2014 was a big year for sports. According to a Nielsen report published in February 2015, more than 70 million Americans consumed sports content on their phone or computer during the third quarter of 2014. The smartphone, being a mobile, internet-ready device, is a perfect fit with the dynamic ethos of the sports world. According to an explanatory note on the report, published on Nielsen's website, between October 2012 and October 2014, the amount of time the average user spent per month on his phone increased by 35%.

Thanks to the development of sports apps, fans are able to view their favorite sports content when and where they want to. According to a survey carried out in late 2014 by Flurry, a company acquired by Yahoo! that specializes in analyzing mobile applications and devices, the time spent on sports applications more than tripled worldwide between August 2013 and August 2014—an increase of 210% — while the total time spent using all applications went up by 65% during the same period.

Sports content is no longer the guarded preserve of television channels. Digital media have become an essential part of the broadcasting of sporting events. I recall that in August 2008, when I was in charge of content partnerships for YouTube in London, I negotiated with the International Olympic Committee the rights for YouTube to broadcast the highlights of the Beijing Olympic Games in 77 countries of Africa, Asia and the Middle East, where no broadcasting agreement had been signed and where the rights were non-exclusive. Our agreement was groundbreaking because it was the first time that the Olympic Games had been made truly accessible throughout the entire world, a feat made possible by YouTube. It was also the first time that a prestigious sports organization had decided to collaborate openly with the online platform.

Mobile applications and online platforms now also enable unique content to be developed and broadcast. According to Jeff Nathenson, Senior Vice-President of Whistle Sports, a multi-channel network (MCN) specializing in digital sports content[1], «*Television isn't necessarily the best location for all sports events. For the big leagues and competitions, television remains an efficient and ideal location for having a shared experience. And those sports will see their share of television licensing fees grow. However, for competitions that have*

1 Interviewed by the authors in December 2014.»

international appeal, but not the same level of ratings impact—say, Olympics sports—they are going to find a bigger and more engaged audience through social media. This requires a different approach and the first step is to embrace the platforms as opposed to avoiding them. »

Athletes also have an active presence on social networks. Cristiano Ronaldo is the athlete with the greatest number of followers on Facebook. With more than 117 million likes, the Portuguese soccer player is also a superstar online.

Fans of course follow news about their sports idols on social media, but they also ask them questions directly, without journalists playing the role of go-betweens. There are no longer filters between fans and the stars who produce content and showcase themselves on the social networks. Consequently, they are showing their fans things they've never shown them before. Social platforms also broaden and strengthen the collaborations between athletes and sponsors, taking them beyond the playing field. In this way, they create closer links between brands and athletes.

« *Social platforms have brought fans and athletes in ever closer proximity* », explains Jeff Nathenson. « *With Instagram there is a chance for an athlete to communicate directly and immediately to his or her fan base across the globe with little or no effort, inviting the fans to see into their amazing lives.* » He adds that, « *What we are seeing is the creation of a new type of athlete/entertainer. Dude Perfect are five guys who never came close to becoming professional athletes themselves. However, their sporting feats—including amazing trick shots—are famous amongst Millennials.* » Dude Perfect is a group of five enthusiasts who practice all kinds of sports, blending athletic feats with comedy. Their videos on YouTube have been viewed more than 2.3 billion times. « *Dude Perfect has the ability to make sports fun and accessible. And for their fans, they are viewed as sporting celebrities perhaps as much as those people who are out on the pitch* », says Nathenson. And that is undoubtedly what explains their success. By way of comparison: Dude Perfect's YouTube channel has about 13.9 million subscribers, while the YouTube channel of the Olympic Games, entitled « *Olympics* », has just 1.6 million.

Garrett Hilbert, Tyler Toney, and Coby Cotton: three of the five athletes of Dude Perfect on stage during the Nickelodeon Kids' choice Sports Awards in 2014 in California.

Link to Dude Perfect's YouTube channel: https://www.youtube.com/user/corycotton

There are also more and more fans who have become enamored of «*fantasy sports*». The trend first emerged in the 1990s but really took off thanks to the development of the internet. In fantasy sports, fans become virtual coaches who put together their imaginary teams based on the performance of real-life players hailing from a wide gamut of professional sports, including soccer, basketball, baseball, football, hockey, golf, etc. The number of websites, applications and magazines on the topic have been multiplying, as has online betting.

«*Social platforms and video gaming can drive interest in a sport. [They] can get people out of the house to watch or even participate in sport*», explains Nathenson. «*For my generation*», he adds, «*video gaming is something completely separate from sport. For the Millennials, it is different.*» The boundary between sports and video games is no longer so clearly defined.

KEY TAKEAWAYS:

Sports fans use more and more applications with sports content. The digital realm has conquered that of sports, and fans are using social networks to communicate with their favorite athletes.

Chapter 14 – The emergence of highly fan-focused media groups

« We want to be doing a billion, 2 billion, 3 billion video views a month, but with news. [...] [W] e won't be the next CNN or ESPN or MTV, we'll be 10 times that size. And I think that's what we're going to do in the next few years. »

Shane Smith, co-founder of Vice,
at TechCrunch Disrupt, May 2014

In the beginning, YouTube frightened traditional media, which saw the platform as a piracy site and tried to undermine it through the filing of various lawsuits. Instead of questioning themselves and imagining a new development model on the groundbreaking platform, the major media groups snubbed YouTube even as it developed into a major social phenomenon.

Since YouTube had a very limited supply of traditional media content, the site developed differently. Internet users, themselves fans, became content creators, launching YouTube channels galore. So it was that YouTube gave rise to its own stars, thereby creating a new genre, a new business model and even new media groups called multi-channel networks (MCNs), which aggregate YouTube channels.

This new type of company was first established in the United States and then in Europe. MCNs work closely with the content creators of the channels they represent in order to grow their audience, improve the quality of their videos, help them to produce content, manage their web media and traditional media communications, monetize videos, negotiate contracts with brands and protect their video rights. In short, MCNs multitask.

With more than 1 billion unique visitors to the platform each month, YouTube has become a medium that cannot be ignored. And now a new economic system is forming around all these web channels, which among other impacts is reintroducing intermediation between fans and stars, which had significantly diminished during the rise of the internet.

Certain MCNs group together YouTube channels specialized in certain areas. Tastemade, for example, focuses on food and travel. StyleHaul brings together more than 6,000 channels dedicated to fashion and cosmetics. And Revision3 highlights content involving new technologies. Other MCNs are more generalist, with a wide variety of web channels in their lineup. Such is the case of AwesomenessTV, Collective Digital Studio and Fullscreen. The latter is one of the best known agencies in the industry. All told, the channels it represents reached more than 7 billion views and over than 700 million subscribers in January 2016.

George Strompolos, CEO & Co-Founder of Fullscreen

Recently, multi-channel networks have attracted the interest of major traditional media groups, which grudgingly and from a remove witnessed their emergence as a major media phenomenon. These traditional media are now trying to position themselves in an industry—online content creation and broadcasting—that until recently they had neglected. They are making numerous acquisitions, as if to make up for lost time and join the digital content race. For example, in 2013 AwesomenessTV was bought for $33 million by DreamWorks Animation, which then sold 25 % of the network to the Hearst Corporation—parent company of Cosmopolitan and Marie-Claire, among many other publications—for $81 million. In 2014, the Walt Disney Company acquired Maker Studios for nearly $1 billion. And RTL Group, a leading European entertainment company, took over StyleHaul, while Discovery Channel took over Revision3.

The relationship between content creators and MCNs is based on an exclusivity contract under which they share the revenue from advertising. According to Patrick Walker[1], the current Director of Media Partnerships, EMEA at Facebook andthe former CEO of Rightster, which is the number one multi-channel network in terms of audience and the fourth largest network in the world, competition between all of the MCNs is fierce: «*If you are in the game of just*

1 Interviewed by the authors in December 2014.

managing YouTube channels on behalf of creators, it's tricky. Margins are getting squeezed because of the competition between so many MCNs that want to work with you. And also new players on the market who are basically passing through revenue from YouTube to get access to the creators for other means to represent the brands. So there is a lot of pressure. The risk with doing everything just on YouTube is that you are too dependent on just one player. The need to diversify is very important. In a world where YouTube margins are getting narrower and there is too much dependence on YouTube, an MCN that doesn't seek diverse distribution across other platforms, other networks, etc., will find itself and its staff in a tricky situation. So yes, the model is sustainable if you are evolving quickly enough to take advantage of platforms where the margins are good and if you can build scalable technology that allows you to do a lot of things. »

Consequently, the wave of buyouts that MCNs are currently undergoing, with a view to subduing the competition, is clearly not about to subside.

Maker Studios, a new web giant

Founded in 2009, Maker Studios is a worldwide network of YouTube channels that provides audiovisual production services for online videos. Since its buyout by the Walt Disney Company in 2014, it has become the third biggest company in terms of audience on the 'net, behind Google and Facebook. Maker Studios attracts more than 10 billion views every month and has more than 650 million subscribers and 60,000 independent creators located in more than 100 countries.

KEY TAKEAWAYS:

A new economic model has emerged: that of the «production company 2.0», i.e., MCNs (multi-channel networks), which promote the stars of social networks and seek out new talent.

Chapter 15 – Fan engagement

#Fans shows how fans have gained a certain power thanks to new technologies and to online platforms, to such an extent that they have revolutionized the media industries and beyond. How can fans be inspired to feel excitement for a star, a song, a brand, a video game, a book or a project? How can their buy-in, their loyalty and their engagement be encouraged? How can advertisers, communications firms and marketing and media professionals successfully target these fans or many potential future enthusiasts? These are all questions one may have about fans' new behaviors, and that all professionals must henceforth ask themselves before targeting Millennials.

Defining « fan engagement »

«*Fan engagement*» is a new concept of the digital era, unlike the previous norms of communication. Three criteria should be considered when interacting with fans and encouraging their buy-in.

1. Medium: Until just a few years ago, the media used to communicate with the bulk of the population were television, radio, the press and billboards. In the digital era, communication with fans happens through smartphones, the web and social networks. Screens—whether on mobile phones, tablets or computers—are becoming the predominant medium. Millennials no longer watch television; they instead surf from platform to platform on their smartphones. TV advertising is therefore becoming ineffective and advertising professionals need to rethink their communications strategy.

2. Format: When TV sets first made their way into people's living rooms, the commercials they broadcasted were little more than radio ads with images. The first TV commercial for Barbie, which was broadcasted in 1959, is a perfect example. Featuring background music, an off-screen voice announcing the doll's price and a few frozen images, it was clearly inspired by well-tried radio techniques. It was therefore necessary to continue inventing the concept of advertising on television. With the advent of the internet there has been a tendency to make the same sort of mistake by showing online ads that are only about 30 seconds long, just like the ones they still broadcast on TV. But in the digital age, this rule no longer makes any sense. With the web, anything is possible. For example, the ads on Vessel, a new video-sharing platform, are no longer than six seconds. In contrast, the ad for the Mercedes-Benz GLA-Class, released in 2013, has a total length of several hours. The traditional rules of

marketing no longer apply. Advertising formats must therefore be reinvented for a digital world. Ads must be relevant and useful for consumers, and not intrusive. It can be completely integrated into content, or even become content itself.

For example, Turkish Airlines launched an ad campaign entitled «*#FortuneTraveller*» on its YouTube channel. It features a number of YouTube stars who are sent to one of the destinations served by the airline in order to vlog, i.e., post a video blog so their fans can follow them on their journey. In this case, the advertising is not hidden, but it leads to the viewing of content.

3. Communication: On television and in magazines, communication is one-way, standardized and highly-regulated, whereas on the internet and social networks, it is two-way, participatory and authentic. On TV, advertisers must contend with shrinking audiences, whereas on smartphones and tablets ads are effective because they are targeted and personalized. Before, the public was an audience. Now the public is composed of fans or even superfans who participate and interact. The challenge for advertisers is no longer to make viewers watch an ad but to get them to share it and make their own versions of it.

Advertisers such as Red Bull and GoPro are becoming content creators themselves. For the brands and stars of the web, today's challenge consists of building a community around themselves.

Making a successful diagnosis

In the relationship between fans and brands, media, stars, etc., new forces are coming into play: technological innovations, globalisation, mobility and the fragmentation of social networks. These four forces require those who wish to communicate with fans to weigh, assess and modify their strategy in order to target Millennials more effectively.

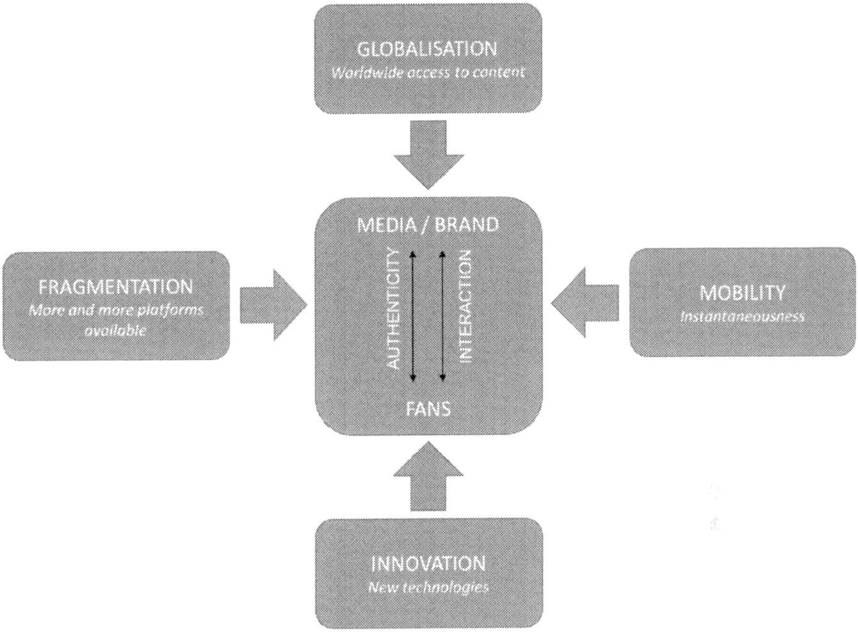

Fans and the 4 forces:

1. Innovation:

New technologies are at the very heart of fan engagement. The advances they represent allow us to improve our lifestyles and the ways in which we consume. The five areas in which key innovations are occurring are data storage (the cloud, etc.), wearable technologies (e.g., the Apple Watch), virtual and augmented reality (e.g., Magic Leap, a startup specializing in augmented reality, funded by Google), 3D printing (e.g., Twindom, which prints figurines in 3D) and robotics, particularly the emergence of drones.

Innovation breeds further innovation and the pace is accelerating. Staying current is a must. Meanwhile, new technologies are becoming ever more affordable. A virtual reality headset only costs a few hundred dollars. In order to stay relevant in terms of communication, technological advances must be anticipated.

Key questions:
- Does your business have the internal ability to anticipate and benefit from technological innovations that could affect it?
- How can your business strategy keep pace with technological change?
- Does your brand have a presence on trend-setting new platforms?
- In the distribution sector, for example, what would be the implications of a virtual reality headset that allows one to visit a store located on the other side of the planet?

2. Globalisation:

With the advent of the internet and platforms such as YouTube, Vine, Instagram, Netflix and Twitter, the obstacles of time and space have been practically eliminated. Global and instantaneous are the new normal, especially since, in the near future, phones will have basic virtual reality features. With just a few taps on the screen, users will be transported to the other end of the world.

The world is within a fingertip's reach. The global success of South Korean singer Psy, with his hit «*Gangnam Style*», is an excellent example of that fact.

Key questions:
- Is your approach global?
- Is your content visual enough to be understood worldwide?
- Does your content need to be translated to be exportable, i.e., to be seen beyond your borders?

3. Mobility / Multitasking:

Fans are mobile, and wherever they are they stay connected. They consume content via their smartphones and tablets while on the move or while watching TV. They multitask. The internet is available to them where and when they want it.

The development of wearable technologies such as smartwatches and smartglasses is allowing users to multitask more than ever. The Apple Watch encourages interaction through its notification system. And Google Glass offers a wealth of possibilities. For example, video conferences could be held using this new kind of glasses.

Key questions:
- Does your site display properly on smartphones and tablets? Google has modified its algorithm to give more visibility in search results to websites that have been optimized for mobile screens.
- Does your content have a presence on social media?
- Does your site or application work with new wearable technologies?

4. Fragmentation:

Social networks are numerous and varied. Fans are no longer satisfied with just one platform. They browse here and there, always on the lookout for more innovative content. Indeed, more and more social platforms are disappearing, while at the same time new ones are constantly being created—from Friendster to MySpace, from Facebook to Instagram...

A few years ago, Snapchat was still on the fringes. Now it is all the rage among teenagers. The newest arrival to the world of social apps is Periscope. This platform, which allows users to broadcast live from their phone cameras, was just bought by Twitter for nearly $100 million.

Key questions:
- How should brands choose their platforms?
- How can one establish a presence on all these new emerging platforms?
- How can relevant content be produced for all these platforms?
- What content should be put on which platforms?
- How can one stay on the lookout for new platforms?

Authenticity and interaction must govern the relationship between fans and those who communicate with them. This communication must be two-way, easy and sincere.

→ How does one achieve authenticity?
- Do you know your fans?
- Does your ad campaign think outside the box?
- Is your communication sincere?
- Have you considered collaborating with web stars? Examples include Lancôme's collaboration with Michelle Phan, Aéropostale's with Bethany Mota and LG's with Zach King. These stars are better known among Millennials than « *offline* » celebrities such as Leonardo

Di Caprio. They therefore have more impact when they appear in ad campaigns targeting the Millennial age group.

→ ***How does one create interaction?***
- Does your communication allow Millennials to express themselves, make comments and share «*likes*»?
- Does your campaign allow for sharing?
- Does your campaign allow fans the possibility of making it their own, of reimagining it in the form of remixes, parodies and new versions? Fans love to pay homage to their favorite stars, the way they did when Disney's animated film Frozen was released and they uploaded a huge number of amateur versions of the famous song «*Let It Go*».

In other words, communication with Millennials must be global, authentic and interactive, as well as compatible with mobile devices and every platform.

The 10 golden rules for creating fan engagement

According to Henri Kaufman[1], the editorial director of the publishing house Éditions Kawa and co-founder of the YouTube channel «*Les Vidéos du Succès*» («*The Videos of Success*») with his associate Pierre-Philippe Cormeraie, aka PPC, some of the keys to having a successful video and YouTube channel are as follows: «*What's important is what happens at the start. It's like a rocket: you have to boost it for a successful lift off and light the fuse. Friends have to share the videos. You also have to keep the tone light and not tire out your viewers. Finally, you have to be tenacious and interactive with your audience.*»

In order to ensure an effective communication campaign that targets Millennials and achieves their buy-in, engagement and loyalty, here are 10 tips:

1. Have an effective editorial strategy

You must always think of your fans, first and foremost. The best way to satisfy them is to post content often. Regular programming is the key to attracting and keeping fans. Consider uploading exclusive content such as interviews, behind-the-scenes videos, etc.

1 Interviewed by the authors in October 2015.

Schedule and create your content around a tentpole event or around holidays such as Christmas, Easter, Mother's and Father's Day, Halloween, Thanksgiving, etc.

Launching a channel, an application or a page on a social network requires the same discipline as that needed to create a traditional television channel: you need a real strategy and real programming. For example, Red Bull and GoPro have become actual content broadcasters. The former has 5.5 million subscribers to its YouTube channel and the latter has more than 4 million, enabling them to reach a wide audience through relevant programming. Their subscriber base is a guaranteed and free audience for them. They have managed to become full-fledged media by becoming creators and broadcasters of content.

Lastly, don't forget to add notes or thumbnails to your videos in order to direct viewers to other web pages and generate traffic.

2. Be mobile

On average, more than 50% of views on YouTube are from mobile phones. Going online is meant to happen on the go, so think about developing your content so that it's adapted to smartphones and tablets.

It is vital for you to have a mobile presence in order to effectively engage with your fanbase while making the most of all the features that smartphones offer, including geolocation, an on-board camera, a touch screen, etc.

If needed, develop an application to provide more advanced features to your superfans and enhance their loyalty.

3. Be global

Your online content needs to be appreciated outside of your home territory and must therefore be understood by a worldwide, globalised audience that does not necessarily speak your language. Here is a perfect example of globalisation: in 2012, Turkish Airlines launched an ad in partnership with the MCN Rightster and two international sports stars: soccer player Lionel Messi and basketball player Kobe Bryant. The two superstars, who are shown together on a plane, barely speak a word but both show off their talents. The ad was posted on YouTube, where it has been viewed more than 100 million times.

If necessary, consider using the subtitling feature provided by YouTube.

4. Be authentic

Michelle Phan, YouTube's makeup star, would never recommend beauty products she doesn't like to her 9 million fans, otherwise she would lose their trust. That's authenticity!

Compared to TV and movie stars, web celebrities make themselves accessible and available to their fans. After all, it was through direct interactions with their fans that they became famous, and they are grateful to them for that. That's why selfies are the best autographs! Their fans are also their friends.

5. Make your content discoverable

In order to get fans, you first have to be seen, to be discovered in the immensity of the web! Getting noticed—in a good way—will attract page views.

The search engines of Google and YouTube must be able to find you in the enormous database they manage. To help them do so, here are a few technical tips: provide complete metadata, tags and hashtags for your videos. Keep in mind that more than 400 hours of video are uploaded to YouTube every minute. Without this information (metadata, tags and hashtags), it's like throwing a message in a bottle into the ocean. This data gives internet users a chance to discover your content.

Add a thumbnail to your YouTube channel and on social networks add photos that make people want to click on them.

Create playlists to organize your content, which will enable you to generate longer content sessions.

Last but not least, use a network of influencers and opinion leaders to make yourself known and promote your channel.

In addition, YouTube, Facebook and Twitter provide user guides for their applications in order to give users the tools and tips they need to break through on the web.
The home page of YouTube's Creator Hub describes the YouTube for Creators benefits program and its mission: «*Express yourself, build a fan base, and turn your creativity into a career.*» Facebook and Twitter have similar pages, which they call Best Practices. These tools may be accessed via the following links:

http://youtube.com/yt/creators/fr/index.html
http://facebook.com/facebookmedia/best-practices#
http://media.twitter.com/best-practices

6. Become an opinion leader yourself

The purpose of fan engagement is to create a community of fans around a star, a brand or a channel. It is therefore necessary to become an opinion leader, a trend-setter and a «*breaker of news*» ... to give other people a voice so that your own voice is listened to even more.

Relaying content of third parties on Facebook or Twitter—provided that it's relevant—helps achieve that end while also generating traffic. Creating YouTube playlists with videos from other creators is another way to become an opinion leader, an influencer.

7. Encourage communication and participation

Consider encouraging the participation of your fans on the internet in order to enhance your visibility and fame. For example, Youtuber Ryan Higa used the occasion of Mother's Day to challenge his fans to send him a video in which they pay homage to their moms. Operation «*#DearMom*» was a huge success on his new personal application, named «*TeeHee*». He soon received hundreds of videos that he sampled to create a compilation. On the day it was uploaded to YouTube, the «*Dear Mom*» video was viewed more than one million times.

Asking fans to contribute content is therefore a way to promote your channel, to get people to talk about you and to attract new fans.

8. Be accessible for your fans

Appearing live, meeting your fans, hugging them, taking selfies with them, responding to their comments, tweets and posts... these have all become standard rituals for celebrities who know how important it is to make themselves accessible. Taylor Swift has understood this perfectly. In 2012, she took part in a live webcast on YouTube during which she revealed the title and cover of her album RED two months before the album's official release. Within a week of its release, the album sold more than 1 million copies.

Content creators also need to make themselves more accessible so that their fans can fund them through online campaigns, using sites such as Indiegogo and Kickstarter.

9. Know your fans

Once you have a loyal fanbase that follows what you publish online, you can start getting to know them better... the better to satisfy them. To do so, you can use the analytical tools made available free of charge by platforms such as YouTube (YouTube Analytics) and Facebook (Insights). These tools will allow you to determine the number of views, the demographics of your audience and their geographic location, the sources of traffic, at what point a viewer stopped watching a video, and a wide variety of other precious information that will allow you to adapt your content accordingly.

An audience should no longer be measured by the GRP (gross rating point), which evaluates the coverage of an ad campaign on the basis of statistics. It should now be measured on the basis of engagement, i.e., the number of likes and shares and the amount of user-generated content (UGC).

10. Take care of your superfans

Their nicknames are the «*Motavators*», the «*Jerhomies*» and the «*Swifties*»: they are the superfans of Bethany Mota, Jérôme Jarre and Taylor Swift. These stars take great care of them and are attentive to their expectations and wishes. Leverage your superfans, too, and give them more content and interactivity: have them take part in creating your content, reward them and offer them an application to enhance their interactions with you.

Conclusion: What does the future hold? Welcome to the world of The Matrix...

And what about tomorrow? What world will we be living in? How could Millennials possibly be even more connected than they are already?

The answer is almost certainly through virtual reality. What until recently was little more than a science-fiction fantasy seems to be materializing quite quickly. Soon we will be able to transport ourselves virtually to the other end of the planet and even to imaginary worlds, all while having an experience that feels quite real.

«*In the past*», explains William Bao Bean, a venture capitalist who invests in new technologies, «*we had three or four screens—TV, phone, PC—but now we are moving beyond screens to full body interaction with technology. We are moving beyond our eyes and fingers on the keyboard to using the entire body to control and interact with new technologies and those technologies are interacting with our entire body. It's a huge change.*»

In this way, our entire bodies will be connected. In the future, technologies, the human body and social interactions will likely be interwoven, thereby enhancing the «*user experience*» even further.

In 2014, to the tune of $2 billion, Facebook treated itself to a gem of a virtual reality company, named Oculus VR. This firm was founded only two years earlier by Palmer Luckey, a young American with a passion for virtual reality, who designed a virtual reality headset called the Oculus Rift. Oculus VR's successful fundraising campaign, which used the Kickstarter crowdfunding site, allowed it to raise more than $2.4 million to develop its technology.

The company is now part of the Facebook family. In a March 2014 post to his Facebook wall, Facebook CEO Mark Zuckerberg announced the acquisition of Oculus, writing «*Oculus's mission is to enable you to experience the impossible. Their technology opens up the possibility of completely new kinds of experiences*», adding that: «*Immersive gaming will be the first, and Oculus already has big plans here that won't be changing and we hope to accelerate. The Rift is highly anticipated by the gaming community, and there's a lot of interest from developers in building for this platform. We're going to focus on helping Oculus build out their product and develop partnerships to support more games. Oculus will continue operating independently within Facebook to achieve this. But this is just the start. After games, we're going to make Oculus a platform for many other experiences. Imagine enjoying a courtside seat at a game, studying in a classroom of students and teachers all over the world or consulting with a doctor face-to-face—just by putting on goggles in your home. This is really a new communication platform. By feeling truly present, you can share unbounded spaces and experiences with the people in your life. Imagine sharing not just moments with your friends online, but entire experiences and adventures».*

The VR helmet from Facebook-owned Oculus

In short, what the future holds is a world that is connected even through the most virtual of realities, and lives that are socially rich although at times imaginary.

There are even stars who are virtual, such as the humanoid persona Hatsune Miku. She is a singer known as a «*vocaloid*», i.e., a vocal android. Her voice is produced by speech synthesis software designed in Japan by Yamaha. Her avatar is a teenage girl with long turquoise hair. And it is her fans themselves who write the words to her songs. Hatsune Miku is undoubtedly one of the best known vocaloids. She gives concerts and her Facebook profile has been liked by more than 2.5 million people. What will happen if this phenomenon takes hold outside of Japan? Will we see Michael Jackson or Amy Winehouse «*brought back to life*» or will brand new stars be invented out of thin air?

From fans to superfans and from YouTube to Victorious...

YouTube, Vine and Instagram are amazing applications that allow content creators to meet their audience and allow fans to interact with them. These are platforms for fans in the broadest sense. However, superfans, who have become more addicted than ever to social networks and webstars, have come to hold expectations and make demands that, unfortunately, those platforms can no longer meet.

Superfans want more deeply interactive and involved experiences with their stars. Meanwhile, these celebrities—whose audiences are in the millions and consist of fans and subscribers on a variety of different platforms—are no longer just video creators, bloggers and influencers, but also superstars and even brands. They no longer wish to be limited to renting their audience from platforms, nor to generating weak revenue, as has been the case until now. They aspire to far greater things...

In March 2014, I received an email from the former vice-president of YouTube, who also created YouTube TV, Dean Gilbert. He had left YouTube two years earlier in order to join a prestigious Silicon Valley investment fund called Redpoint Ventures. This fund has invested in a number of companies that are now famous, such as Netflix and Tastemade. A few days later, we spoke. Dean told me about a high-potential startup he had invested in that was launched by a former Google executive and a «*serial entrepreneur*». This company, which is called Victorious, allows digital-native content creators—e.g., Michelle Phan and Ryan Higa, to name the most famous among them—to share with their fans and for their fans to interact with them via mobile applications under their own name and brand.

Dean explained to me that these apps will contain a great deal of rich content and highly advanced features. The idea won me over. Following a number of meetings with the founders of Victorious, in the small house in Santa Monica where they set up their offices, they proposed that I work for them as the Vice President of their international division, in charge of developing the company in Europe, Asia and Latin America. The startup has already raised tens of millions of dollars from major investment funds such as Kleiner Perkins (the fund that invested in Google and Amazon), Redpoint Ventures, Lowercase Capital and Bertelsmann Investissement, as well as from the two biggest talent agencies—William Morris and UTA—and

Elisabeth Murdoch, the daughter of media magnate Rupert Murdoch, the founder of News Corp. I managed the International operations of Victorious from March 2015 to March 2016.

A new revolution is underway: encouraged by superfans, superstars are becoming media companies themselves, rivaling the biggest television networks. They have their own audience and their own content aggregated on a single platform, including videos, photos, GIFs, polls, articles and more.

This is tantamount to recreating a social network around a specific celebrity. Imagine YouTube, Instagram, Vine and Twitter joined together in a single application under a star's name! It's a simple and effective way for celebrities to sustain and grow the community of fans that their success and brand rely on.

This type of application will allow those stars who have become brands to generate revenue beyond advertising income from micropayments (paid stickers) and subscriptions.

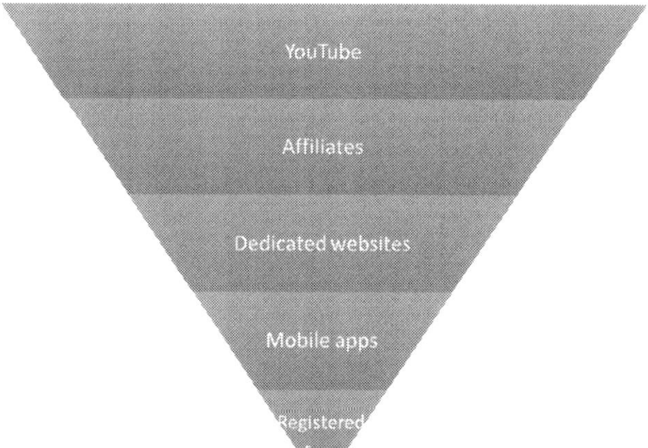

The Fan Engagement Funnel

How can we visualize fan engagement, devotion or loyalty? In order to better understand the idea behind the fan engagement funnel, let's imagine that YouTube is a big multi-brand department store like Macy's or a big-box retailer like Target and that your mobile application is a single-brand store. The two coexist in harmony. A brand can have its own corner inside a Macy's and at the same time have a dedicated boutique on the same street. In this way, it can benefit from the traffic generated by department stores and also the impulse buying of those shoppers. The brand can choose to tailor its own store to its most loyal customers or « *superfans* » as it were.

Platforms such as YouTube, Vine and Instagram have a wide audience and allow one to build a vast fanbase. But it is also important to have a mobile application that fosters a more intimate and exclusive relationship with one's most loyal fans. YouTube provides low monetization from a wide audience, whereas an application provides high monetization from a more concentrated audience.

YouTube stars such as Ryan Higa and Michelle Phan have already used Victorious to produce their own name-brand applications. Who will be the next stars to have their own app? Who will the social networks of the future revolve revolve around?

And who knows? Perhaps one day, you too will have your own personal app, your own media platform!

USEFUL WEBSITES

Online video industry news:

- Tubefilter. http://tubefilter.com/
- VideoInk. http://thevideoink.com/

Rankings and statistics:

- Social Blade. http://socialblade.com/

Statistics on YouTube, Twitch and Instagram.

- Socialbakers. http://socialbakers.com/

Statistics on Twitter, Facebook and Google+.

- App Annie. http://appannie.com/

Statistics on the performance of mobile applications.

Technology and startup news:

- TechCrunch. http://techcrunch.com
- Tech in Asia. http://techinasia.com/

The equivalent of TechCrunch for Asia.

- Gigaom. http://gigaom.com/
- WSJ.D http://wsj.com/news/technology
- Mashable. http://mashable.com/
- Engadget. http://engadget.com/
- Gizmodo. http://gizmodo.com/
- Wired. http://wired.com/

The site of the American technology magazine.

- The Next Web. http://thenextweb.com/
- Re/code. http://recode.net/

Media and entertainment industry news:

- Variety. http://variety.com/
- The Hollywood Reporter. http://hollywoodreporter.com/

Advertising:

- Advertising Age. http://adage.com/
- Campaign Asia. http://campaignasia.com/

EVENTS AND CONFERENCES

For web fans:

- VidCon (Anaheim, CA). http://vidcon.com/

The most important event for web fans and creators, founded by John Green.

- South by Southwest (SXSW) (Austin, TX). http://sxsw.com/

Began as a music-industry event and is now also a conference for the media and digital industries.

- Streamy Awards. http://streamys.org/

The equivalent of the Oscars for online video.

- Comic-Con (San Diego, CA). http://comic-con.org/

World conference for the fans of superheroes and fantasy characters.

- TwitchCon (San Francisco, CA). http://twitchcon.com/

World conference for the fans of video games.

- YouTube Fanfest (multiple cities worldwide). http://youtubefanfest.com/

The equivalent of VidCon outside of the United States.

- Summer in the City (London, UK). http://sitc-event.co.uk/

The British equivalent of VidCon.

- Video Days (Berlin and Cologne, Germany). http://videodays.eu/

The German equivalent of VidCon.

- Vidéo City (Paris, France). http://videocityparis.com/

The French equivalent of VidCon, organized by M6, Mixicom and Canal+.

Conferences for media industry professionals:

- Cannes Lions (Cannes, France). http://canneslions.com/

Conference for the advertising industry.

- MipTV & MIPCOM (Cannes, France). http://miptv.com/ and http://mipcom.com/

International conference for the media industry.

- Midem (Cannes, France). http://midem.com/

International conference for the music industry.

- Mobile World Congress (Barcelona, Spain). http://mobileworldcongress.com/

International conference for the mobile device industry.

- NATPE (Miami, FL). http://natpe.com/

Media conference targeting the American market.

- Kidscreen Summit (Miami, FL). http://summit.kidscreen.com/

Conference the children's content industry.

- All That Matters (Singapore). http://allthatmatters.asia/

The equivalent of South by Southwest for Asia.

- CASBAA Convention (Hong Kong). http://casbaa.com/events/events-calendar

Conference for the television industry in Asia.

- Spikes Asia (Singapore). http://spikes.asia/home/

The equivalent of Cannes Lions for Asia.

- ad : tech (multiple cities). http://ad-tech.com/

Conference for the digital advertising industry.

Conferences for web professionals:

- LeWeb (Paris, France). http://leweb.co/
- HUBFORUM (Paris, France). http://hubforum.com/
- WSJDLive. http://wsjdlive.wsj.com/
- TechCrunch Disrupt (USA, United Kingdom, China). http://techcrunch.com/event-type/disrupt/
- Tech in Asia Conference (Singapore). http://events.techinasia.com/

Chaîne YouTube #FANS:

- www.hashtag-fans.com

ACKNOWLEDGMENTS

I would like to thank everyone who collaborated with me on this book, starting with my former colleagues at YouTube, Patrick Walker and Jeff Nathenson, as well as Yannick Bolloré, Michael Peters, Robert Wolcott, Fabian Manzano, Zach King, Jadon Gauthier, Jonathan Pardo, Bernie Cho, Ted Wright, William Bao Bean, Gabriel Segré, Joachim Roncin, John Wood, Kiera Stevens and Hannah Herrmann.

My thanks also go to Jasper Donat, who supported us, introduced us to many people and gave us the opportunity to promote the book during the All That Matters conference in Singapore in May 2015.

Special thanks to Jean-Marc Tassetto, who agreed without hesitation to write the foreword to #FANS.

Thanks as well to Henri Kaufman and Éditions Kawa, who believed in our project at a time when we thought we might have to self-publish our book on the web.

Loving thanks to my late grandfather, Jacques Souplet, as well as to my parents, Marie-Christine and Olivier Zameczkowski, for having inspired me and made me want to work in this exciting industry.

Thank you to my mentors, Dean Gilbert, Chris Maxcy, Christophe Muller, Patrick Walker, Gautam Anand and Caroline Lang, as well as to my former partners at Victorious, Sam Rogoway, Bing Chen and Mike Todd. I have learned so much with you.

Thank you to Nicolas Giraudon and Julien Bally for their advice and encouragement.

Thank you to Françoise and Charles Prins and to Anne-Isabelle Pain for their precious proofreading.

Thank you to Elena Zameczkowski for lending her teenage perspective to our book.

Thank you to my wife, Agnès, whom I am so fortunate to have by my side and who has always supported my most ambitious projects, including the writing of this book.

Thank you to our respective families for their support.

Last but not least, I would like to give special thanks to my co-author and friend, Colombe Prins, who agreed to follow me into this project with complete confidence. Bravo!

BIBLIOGRAPHY

CHAPTER 1 - Technologies: a new tool for fans

- http://latribune.fr/technos-medias/medias/20150101trib771c1489c/la-television-de-demain-passera-par-internet.html
- http://wsj.com/articles/pay-tv-cord-cutting-accelerates-1415321442
- http://mashable.com/2011/02/19/youtube-facts/
- http://variety.com/2015/digital/news/netflix-tops-57-million-subscribers-in-q4-as-u-s-growth-slows-1201409712/
- https://thinkwithgoogle.com/articles/online-video-mobile-marketing-strategy.html
- http://timewarner.com/newsroom/press-releases/2014/10/15/hbo-chairman-and-ceo-richard-plepler-announces-hbo-to-offer-a
- https://rt.com/news/durov-resigns-vkontakte-social-904/

CHAPTER 2 - Who are the new fans?

- http://pewresearch.org/fact-tank/2015/01/16/this-year-millennials-will-overtake-baby-boomers/
- http://insights.buzzfeed.com/industry-trends-2014/
- http://newyorker.com/magazine/2014/12/15/hollywood-vine
- http://ssl.gstatic.com/think/docs/introducing-gen-c-the-youtube-generation_research-studies.pdf
- http://inspiritfoundation.org/files/6214/0258/2613/Youtube-video-insights-stats-data-trends_research-studies.pdf
- http://thinkwithgoogle.com/articles/meet-gen-c-youtube-generation-in-own-words.html
- http://statista.com/statistics/272014/global-social-networks-ranked-by-number-of-users/
- http://newsweek.com/2014/10/31/youtube-creates-its-own-celebrities-complete-screaming-fans-279586.html
- http://thinkwithgoogle.com/articles/youtube-insights-stats-data-trends-vol7.html
- http://thinkwithgoogle.com/articles/engagement-project-new-normal.html

- http://independent.co.uk/life-style/gadgets-and-tech/features/unboxing-the-new-geek-porn-1333955.html

CHAPTER 3 - How do fans in turn become stars?

- http://newyorker.com/magazine/2014/12/15/hollywood-vine
- http://dailymail.co.uk/femail/article-2777511/Forget-footballer-actress-young-Brits-dream-job-YouTube-star-judging-teen-vloggers-success-s-hardly-surprising.html
- http://variety.com/2015/digital/news/youtubers-teen-survey-ksi-pewdiepie-1201544882/
- http://variety.com/2014/digital/news/netflix-picks-up-camp-takota-from-youtube-stars-grace-helbig-mamrie-hart-and-hannah-hart-1201364772/
- http://adweek.com/news/technology/how-youtubes-hottest-personalities-are-becoming-offline-superstars-161307
- http://recode.net/2014/10/27/michelle-phan-youtube-star-to-startup-founder/
- http://recode.net/2014/10/27/michelle-phan-youtube-star-to-startup-founder/
- http://lindseystirling.com/about/
- http://youtube.com/user/HIKAKIN
- http://adweek.com/news/technology/jerome-jarre-talks-squirrels-and-schools-brands-vine-160108
- http://businessinsider.sg/rosanna-pansino-nerdy-nummies-2014-6/#.VNsTNVoRI1N
- http://forbes.com/sites/natalierobehmed/2015/10/05/how-michelle-phan-built-a-500-million-company/

CHAPTER 4 - Fans: overcoming the barriers of time and space

- http://youtube.com/user/JimmyKimmelLive
- http://bbc.com/news/world-asia-32811867
- http://theguardian.com/technology/2014/apr/08/youtube-fanbases-jimmy-fallon-psy

CHAPTER 5 – Fans: redefining the music industry

- http://news.spotify.com/se/2014/11/11/2-billion-and-counting/
- http://latimes.com/entertainment/envelope/cotown/la-et-ct-youtube-music-streaming-20141113-story.html#page=1
- http://newyorker.com/science/maria-konnikova/how-frozen-took-over-the-world

CHAPTER 6 - The movie and publishing industries are adapting to fans' tastes

- http://time.com/3615753/zoella-girl-online-record-sales/
- http://bbc.co.uk/newsbeat/article/30305855/zoellas-book-girl-online-outsells-jk-rowling
- http://theguardian.com/technology/2014/oct/09/youtube-zoella-mental-health-charity-mind
- http://washingtonpost.com/blogs/style-blog/wp/2014/06/04/the-fault-in-our-stars-by-the-numbers-just-how-huge-is-this-movie-going-to-be/
- http://variety.com/2014/digital/news/fault-in-our-stars-social-media-1201215243/
- http://valeursactuelles.com/culture/john-green-lauteur-de-nos-etoiles-contraires-au-firmament-47432
- http://variety.com/2014/digital/news/netflix-picks-up-camp-takota-from-youtube-stars-grace-helbig-mamrie-hart-and-hannah-hart-1201364772/

CHAPTER 7 – Fans: revolutionizing the advertising industry

- http://adage.com/article/media/digital-overtake-tv-ad-spending-years-forrester/295694/
- http://ft.com/intl/cms/s/0/377f7054-81ef-11e4-b9d0-00144feabdc0.html#axzz3PzTkjBut
- http://youtube.com/watch? v=uw217lO3weY
- http://youtube.com/watch? v=0_Jie5yNJ4A

- http://adweek.com/news/technology/meet-youtube-stars-brands-love-103733
- http://mashable.com/2012/12/19/red-bull-content-marketing/
- http://tubefilter.com/2013/08/13/kurt-hugo-schneider-sam-tsui-coke/
- http://adweek.com/videowatch/youtube-artist-kurt-hugo-schneiders-mesmerizing-coke-video-saw-high-engagement-152171
- http://adweek.com/news/technology/top-10-branded-videos-lg-s-spot-hits-gold-using-vine-star-160913
- http://finance.yahoo.com/blogs/driven/bullied-to-bank--bethany-mota-s-youtube-empire-133655143.html

CHAPTER 8 - Fans are gamers

- http://venturebeat.com/2014/06/24/gamer-globe-the-top-100-countries-by-2014-game-revenue/
- http://wsj.com/articles/gaming-no-longer-a-mans-world-1408464249
- http://newzoo.com/insights/global-games-market-will-reach-102-9-billion-2017-2/
- http://riotgames.com/our-games
- http://cbsnews.com/videos/pay-for-play-twitch-turns-gaming-into-spectator-sport/
- http://forbes.com/sites/insertcoin/2014/01/27/riots-league-of-legends-reveals-astonishing-27-million-daily-players-67-million-monthly/
- http://blogs.wsj.com/digits/2015/01/29/twitchs-viewers-reach-100-million-a-month/
- http://businesswire.com/news/home/20150220005060/en/Twitch-Announces-TwitchCon-2015#.VXUPresRkza
- http://wsj.com/articles/youtube-star-plays-videogames-earns-4-million-a-year-1402939896

CHAPTER 9 – Fans become journalists

- http://fortune.com/2014/02/27/vice-unveils-dedicated-news-site-fact-checkers-and-all-for-generation-y/

- http://iemed.org/observatori-fr/arees-danalisi/arxius-adjunts/anuari/med.2012/mourtada% 20salem_fr.pdf
- http://mashable.com/2012/11/05/sandy-instagram-record/
- http://inaglobal.fr/numerique/article/buzzfeed-un-media-comme-un-autre-7946
- http://buzzfeed.com/advertise
- http://lemonde.fr/international/article/2012/10/19/wael-ghonim-heraut-facebook-de-la-revolution-egyptienne_1778301_3210.html
- http://blogs.wsj.com/dispatch/2012/10/30/on-social-media-sandys-wake-captured-in-photos/
- http://lemonde.fr/technologies/article/2012/10/31/les-reseaux-sociaux-outils-contre-la-tempete-sandy_1783579_651865.html
- http://lapresse.ca/arts/medias/201309/18/01-4690578-storyful-lagence-de-presse-du-xxie-siecle.php
- http://telerama.fr/medias/vice-ou-la-trajectoire-d-un-ovni-de-l-info,118342.php
- https://euronewsinside.wordpress.com/2014/02/07/euronews-worlds-1-on-youtube/

CHAPTER 10 – When celebrities are funded by fans

- http://youtube.com/watch? v=xMj_P_6H69g
- http://forbes.com/sites/chancebarnett/2014/08/29/crowdfunding-sites-in-2014/
- http://theguardian.com/media/2012/sep/26/amanda-palmer-future-of-music
- http://tubefilter.com/2014/02/06/freddie-wong-indiegogo-kickstarter-vghs/

CHAPTER 11 – Fans: champions for a cause

- http://newsroom.fb.com/news/2014/08/the-ice-bucket-challenge-on-facebook/
- http://nytimes.com/2014/08/18/business/ice-bucket-challenge-has-raised-millions-for-als-association.html?_r=0
- http://nbcnews.com/feature/making-a-difference/striking-out-als-ice-bucket-challenge-brings-flood-donations-n177896
- http://mashable.com/2013/11/18/batkid-numbers/
- http://nytimes.com/2009/06/23/world/middleeast/23neda.html?_r=0
- http://mashable.com/2015/01/09/jesuischarlie-hashtag-popularity/
- http://lemonde.fr/m-actu/article/2015/01/09/je-suis-charlie-c-est-lui_4552523_4497186.html
- http://lemonde.fr/pixels/article/2015/01/07/sur-internet-vague-mondiale-d-emotion-apres-la-tuerie-de-charlie-hebdo_4550975_4408996.html

CHAPTER 12 - Fans take an interest in politics

- http://washingtonpost.com/politics/in-president-obamas-white-house-some-traditions-give-way-to-modern-technology/2014/07/06/431864be-eb51-11e3-9f5c-9075d5508f0a_story.html
- http://youtube.com/watch?v=GbR6iQ62v9k
- http://forbes.com/sites/anuraghunathan/2014/07/11/narendra-modi-is-asias-most-followed-leader-on-twitter/

CHAPTER 13 – Fans and their love for sports

- http://nielsen.com/us/en/insights/news/2015/the-year-in-sports-digital-steps-up-to-the-plate.html
- http://velocityagency.com/sports-fans-overtake-digital-media-velocity-agency-new-orleans/
- http://emarketer.com/Article/Sports-Apps-Win-Over-Fans/1011434

- http://forbes.com/sites/kurtbadenhausen/2014/06/11/cristiano-ronaldo-leads-the-biggest-athletes-on-social-media/
- http://cbc.ca/news/technology/ioc-strikes-deal-with-youtube-to-bring-olympics-online-1.746899
- http://sportsbusinessdaily.com/Journal/Issues/2014/10/13/Research-and-Ratings/Sports-Fan-Engagement-Study.aspx

CHAPTER 14 - The emergence of highly fan-focused media groups

- http://redef.com/original/how-youtube-mcns-are-conquering-hollywood? curator=MediaREDEF&utm_content=buffer663f2&utm_medium=social&utm_source=linkedin.com&utm_campaign=buffer
- http://variety.com/2014/digital/news/after-disney-maker-deal-more-deals-in-store-for-multichannel-networks-1201145205/
- http://forbes.com/sites/dorothypomerantz/2014/04/01/with-disney-buying-maker-do-all-big-media-companies-need-to-up-their-youtube-game/

PHOTO CREDITS

UNITED STATES, New York: NEW YORK, NY - APRIL 23: Michelle Phan (C) posing with fans at the Unleash YouTube Event with stars Michelle Phan, Rosanna Pansino and Bethany Mota on April 23, 2014 in New York City. Dimitrios Kambouris/Getty Images for YouTube/AFP.

UNITED STATES, CENTURY CITY: CENTURY CITY, CA - NOVEMBER 20: (L-R) Josh Boone, Ansel Elgort, Shailene Woodley and John Green attending 20th Century Fox Home Entertainment's The Fault In Our Stars reunion and bench dedication ceremony at a Fox Studio lot on November 20, 2014 in Century City, California. Valerie Macon/Getty Images/AFP.

UNITED STATES, New York: NEW YORK, NY - MAY 5: Shane Smith, co-founder and CEO of VICE, speaking at TechCrunch Disrupt NY 2014 - Day 1 on May 5, 2014 in New York City. Brian Ach/Getty Images for TechCrunch/AFP.

UNITED STATES, San Francisco: SAN FRANCISCO, CA - NOVEMBER 15: Larry Baer, CEO of the San Francisco Giants, and the team's mascot, Lou Seal, escort leukemia survivor Miles, age 5, dressed as BatKid, together with Batman, to the outfield to see a message on the scoreboard as part of a Make-A-Wish foundation fulfillment held at AT&T Park on November 15, 2013 in San Francisco. The Make-A-Wish Greater Bay Area Foundation turned the city into Gotham City for Miles by creating a day-long event bringing his wish to be BatKid to life. Ramin Talaie/Getty Images/AFP.

UNITED STATES, Chicago: A YouTube video of US President-elect Barack Obama's weekly radio address is seen on a computer screen in Chicago on November 22, 2008. AFP PHOTO/Saul LOEB.

UNITED STATES, Los Angeles: LOS ANGELES, CA - JULY 17: Olympic snowboarder Kelly Clark; comedians Garrett Hilbert, Tyler Toney and Coby Cotton of Dude Perfect; and TV personality George Lopez speak onstage during Nickelodeon Kids' Choice Sports Awards 2014 at UCLA's Pauley Pavilion on July 17, 2014 in Los Angeles, California. Kevin Winter/Getty Images/AFP.

UNITED STATES, New York: NEW YORK, NY - MAY 04: George Strompolos attends the Fullscreen NewFront 2015 event at Highline Stages on May 4, 2015 in New York City. Craig Barritt/Getty Images for Fullscreen/AFP.

UNITED KINGDOM, London: LONDON, ENGLAND - MARCH 12: Westfield, introducing the world's first Oculus Rift Virtual Reality headsets ahead of «*Future Fashion*», an immersive pop-up experience held at Westfield London on March 12, 2015 in London, England. Future Fashion will take place at Westfield London from March 27th to 29th and at Westfield Stratford City from April 2 to 4. (Photo by Tim P. Whitby/Getty Images for Westfield).

GERMANY, Berlin: Numerous fans cheering on YouTube stars during their live performances in Arena Halle in Berlin, Germany, May 2, 2015. Various YouTube stars showing off their talent at the end of the first VideoDays 2015. Photo: PAUL ZINKEN/dpa.

UNITED STATES, PASADENA: PASADENA, CA - SEPTEMBER 13: Fans watch Dylan Dauzat pay tribute to Connor Franta and JC Caylen for inspiring him to join YouTube at Fullscreens INTOUR at Pasadena Convention Center on September 13, 2014 in Pasadena, California. Jesse Grant/Getty Images for Fullscreen/AFP.

FRANCE, Paris: A magnifying glass shows the number of times that viewers have watched South Korean rapper Psy's video for «*Gangnam Style*» on YouTube. Date: December 21, 2012. Psy's «*Gangnam Style*» became the first video to hit a billion views on YouTube, marking a fresh milestone in the global craze for the South Korean rapper and his horse-riding dance. The view counter attached to «*Gangnam Style*», which was posted on the video-sharing site on July 15, 2012, clicked over into 10 figures at around 3: 50 PM GMT, confirming its status as the most viewed video in the site's history. AFP PHOTO/THOMAS COEX.

UNITED STATES, Hoboken: HOBOKEN, NJ - OCTOBER 24: Recording artists Fabian Manzano, Alejandro Manzano and Daniel Manzano of Boyce Avenue, performing during Juicy Fruit Presents Boyce Avenue Powered by Pandora on October 24, 2014 in Hoboken, New Jersey. Bennett Raglin/Getty Images for Pandora/AFP.

CANADA, Toronto: TORONTO, ON - AUGUST 26: YouTube celebrity Bethany «*Macbarbie07*» Mota hosting an exclusive meet-and-greet at the Aéropostale store in Toronto Eaton Center on August 26, 2013 in Toronto, Canada. George Pimentel/Getty Images for Aeropostale/ AFP.

UNITED STATES, Manhattan Beach: Daerek «*LemonNation*» Hart (R) and teammate Zachary «*Sneaky*» Scuderi of team Cloud 9 follow the action during the live taping of the League of Legends North American Championship Series Spring Round Robin Competition, at the MBS Media Campus in Manhattan Beach, California, on February 22, 2014. League of Legends, one of the world's most popular multiplayer online arena battle video games, has a fully professional competitive league and a top prize of one million dollars. AFP PHOTO / ROBYN BECK

UNITED KINGDOM, Glastonbury: US singer Amanda Palmer, performing on the Pyramid Stage on the third day of the Glastonbury Festival of Contemporary Performing Arts near Glastonbury, southwest England on June 28, 2013. The festival attracts 170,000 party-goers to a dairy farm in Somerset, and this year's tickets sold out within two hours of going on sale. The Rolling Stones performed at the festival for the first time, headlining on Saturday night. AFP PHOTO/ANDREW COWIE.

Contents

EDITIONS
kawa

www.editions-kawa.com

Publication director :
Xavier WARGNIER

www.facebook.com/xavierwargnier
http://twitter.com/xavierwargnier
http://fr.linkedin.com/in/xavierwargnier

Follow us :
http://www.youtube.com/user/KawaEditions
http://www.facebook.com/editions.kawa

Printed in France by SOBOOK :
45 rue Rollin 59100 ROUBAIX
ISBN : 978-2-36778-110-5
Dépôt légal : Février 2017

Editions Kawa
88, Chemin des Perrières - 74290 Bluffy - France
www.editions-kawa.com

Editorial director
Henri Kaufman

Translation :
Martin Hoffman

Room to Read®

Graphic design
Guillaume Monsigny
www.gm-design.fr

www.editions-kawa.com

Made in United States
Orlando, FL
05 November 2026

90241896R00087